Lecture Notes in Computer Science　14204

Founding Editors

Gerhard Goos
Juris Hartmanis

The series Lecture Notes in Computer Science (LNCS), including its subseries Lecture Notes in Artificial Intelligence (LNAI) and Lecture Notes in Bioinformatics (LNBI), has established itself as a medium for the publication of new developments in computer science and information technology research, teaching, and education.

LNCS enjoys close cooperation with the computer science R & D community, the series counts many renowned academics among its volume editors and paper authors, and collaborates with prestigious societies. Its mission is to serve this international community by providing an invaluable service, mainly focused on the publication of conference and workshop proceedings and postproceedings. LNCS commenced publication in 1973.

Min Luo · Liang-Jie Zhang

Editors

Cloud Computing – CLOUD 2023

16th International Conference
Held as Part of the Services Conference Federation, SCF 2023
Shenzhen, China, December 17–18, 2023
Proceedings

 Springer

Editors
Min Luo
Georgia Institute of Technology
Atlanta, GA, USA

Liang-Jie Zhang ⓘ
Shenzhen Entrepreneurship and Innovation
Federation
Shenzhen, China

ISSN 0302-9743 ISSN 1611-3349 (electronic)
Lecture Notes in Computer Science
ISBN 978-3-031-51708-2 ISBN 978-3-031-51709-9 (eBook)
https://doi.org/10.1007/978-3-031-51709-9

This Springer imprint is published by the registered company Springer Nature Switzerland AG
The registered company address is: Gewerbestrasse 11, 6330 Cham, Switzerland

Paper in this product is recyclable.

Preface

As the pioneering conference exclusively focused on cloud computing, the International Conference on Cloud Computing (CLOUD) serves as a prominent global platform for researchers and industry professionals to share the most recent foundational breakthroughs in the theory and application of cloud computing. It facilitates the exploration of emerging research areas and the shaping of the future landscape of cloud computing. Every aspect related to cloud computing resonates with the overarching theme of the CLOUD conference.

CLOUD 2023 was a member of the Services Conference Federation (SCF). SCF 2023 had the following 10 collocated service-oriented sister conferences: 2023 International Conference on Web Services (ICWS 2023), 2023 International Conference on Cloud Computing (CLOUD 2023), 2023 International Conference on Services Computing (SCC 2023), 2023 International Conference on Big Data (BigData 2023), 2023 International Conference on AI & Mobile Services (AIMS 2023), 2023 International Conference on Metaverse (METAVERSE 2023), 2023 International Conference on Internet of Things (ICIOT 2023), 2023 International Conference on Cognitive Computing (ICCC 2023), 2023 International Conference on Edge Computing (EDGE 2023), and 2023 International Conference on Blockchain (ICBC 2023). As the founding member of SCF, the first International Conference on Web Services (ICWS) was held in June 2003 in Las Vegas, USA. Meanwhile, the First International Conference on Web Services - Europe 2003 (ICWS-Europe'03) was held in Germany in October, 2003. ICWS-Europe'03 was an extended event of the 2003 International Conference on Web Services (ICWS 2003) in Europe. In 2004, ICWS-Europe became the European Conference on Web Services (ECOWS), which was held in Erfurt, Germany.

This volume presents the accepted papers for the 2023 International Conference on Cloud Computing (CLOUD 2023), held in Shenzhen, Guangdong, China during December 17–18, 2023. For this conference, each paper was reviewed by three independent members of the International Program Committee in a single-blind review process. After carefully evaluating their originality and quality, 8 papers were accepted.

We are pleased to thank the authors whose submissions and participation made this conference possible. We also want to express our thanks to the Program Committee members, for their dedication in helping organize the conference and review the submissions.

Finally, we would like to thank operation team members Jing Zeng, Yishuang Ning, Sheng He, and Bo Hu for their excellent work in organizing this conference. We look forward to your great contributions as a volunteer, author, and conference participant in the fast-growing worldwide services innovations community.

December 2023   Min Luo
                                                                      Liang-Jie Zhang

Organization

Program Chair

Min Luo   Georgia Tech, USA

Services Conference Federation (SCF 2023)

General Chairs

Ali Arsanjani   Google, USA
Wu Chou   Essenlix Corporation, USA

Coordinating Program Chair

Liang-Jie Zhang   Shenzhen Entrepreneurship & Innovation
                                    Federation, China

CFO and International Affairs Chair

Min Luo   Georgia Tech, USA

Operation Committee

Jing Zeng   China Gridcom Co., Ltd., China
Yishuang Ning   Tsinghua University, China
Sheng He   Tsinghua University, China

Steering Committee

Calton Pu (Co-chair)   Georgia Tech, USA
Liang-Jie Zhang (Co-chair)   Shenzhen Entrepreneurship & Innovation
                                    Federation, China

CLOUD 2023 Program Committee

Roberto Di Pietro	Hamad Bin Khalifa University, Qatar
Sanjay Patel	Nirma University, India
Byungchul Tak	Kyungpook National University, South Korea
Yingwei Wang	University of Prince Edward Island, Canada
Yuehua Wang	Texas A & M University - Commerce, USA
Hailu Xu	California State University, Long Beach, USA
R. K. N. Sai Krishna	Yugabyte, USA
Rüdiger Schulze	IBM Germany Research & Development GmbH, Germany
Feng Chen	Louisiana State University, USA
Haopeng Chen	Shanghai Jiao Tong University, China
Jingshu Chen	Oakland University, USA
Shahram Ghandeharizadeh	University of Southern California, USA
Supratik Mukhopadhyay	Louisiana State University, USA
Jun Shen	University of Wollongong, Australia

Conference Sponsor – Services Society

The Services Society (S2) is a non-profit professional organization that has been created to promote worldwide research and technical collaboration in services innovations among academia and industrial professionals. Its members are volunteers from industry and academia with common interests. S2 is registered in the USA as a "501(c) organization", which means that it is an American tax-exempt nonprofit organization. S2 collaborates with other professional organizations to sponsor or co-sponsor conferences and to promote an effective services curriculum in colleges and universities. S2 initiates and promotes a "Services University" program worldwide to bridge the gap between industrial needs and university instruction.

The Services Sector accounted for 79.5% of the GDP of the USA in 2016. The Services Society has formed 5 Special Interest Groups (SIGs) to support technology and domain-specific professional activities.

- Special Interest Group on Services Computing (SIG-SC)
- Special Interest Group on Big Data (SIG-BD)
- Special Interest Group on Cloud Computing (SIG-CLOUD)
- Special Interest Group on Artificial Intelligence (SIG-AI)
- Special Interest Group on Metaverse (SIG-Metaverse)

About the Services Conference Federation (SCF)

As the founding member of the Services Conference Federation (SCF), the first International Conference on Web Services (ICWS) was held in June 2003 in Las Vegas, USA. Meanwhile, the First International Conference on Web Services - Europe 2003 (ICWS-Europe'03) was held in Germany in October, 2003. ICWS-Europe 2003 was an extended event of the 2003 International Conference on Web Services (ICWS 2003) in Europe. In 2004, ICWS-Europe became the European Conference on Web Services (ECOWS), which was held in Erfurt, Germany. To celebrate its 21st birthday, SCF 2023 phase-I was held on September 23–26, 2023, in Honolulu, Hawaii, USA and SCF 2023 phase-II was held on December 17–18, 2023, in Shenzhen, Guangdong, China.

In the past 20 years, the ICWS community has been expanded from Web engineering innovations to scientific research for the whole services industry. The service delivery platforms have been expanded to mobile platforms, Internet of Things, cloud computing, and edge computing. The services ecosystem has gradually been enabled, value added, and intelligence embedded through enabling technologies such as big data, artificial intelligence, and cognitive computing. In the coming years, all transactions with multiple parties involved will be transformed to blockchain.

Based on technology trends and best practices in the field, SCF will continue to serve as the umbrella code name for all services-related conferences. SCF 2023 defines the future of New ABCDE (AI, Blockchain, Cloud, big Data, Everything is connected), which enable IOT and take us into the 5G for Services Era. SCF 2023's 10 co-located theme topic conferences all centered around "services", while each focused on exploring different themes (web-based services, cloud-based services, Big Data-based services, services innovation lifecycle, AI-driven ubiquitous services, blockchain-driven trust service-ecosystems, industry-specific services and applications, and emerging service-oriented technologies). SCF includes 10 service-oriented conferences: ICWS, CLOUD, SCC, BigData Congress, AIMS, METAVERSE, ICIOT, EDGE, ICCC, and ICBC. The SCF 2023 members are listed as follows:

[1] The 2023 International Conference on Web Services (ICWS 2023, http://icws. org/) was the flagship theme-topic conference for Web-based services, featuring Web services modeling, development, publishing, discovery, composition, testing, adaptation, and delivery, as well as the latest API standards.
[2] The 2023 International Conference on Cloud Computing (CLOUD 2023, http://thecloudcomputing.org/) was the flagship theme-topic conference for modeling, developing, publishing, monitoring, managing, and delivering XaaS (everything as a service) in the context of various types of cloud environments.
[3] The 2023 International Conference on Big Data (BigData 2023, http://bigdat acongress.org/) was the emerging theme-topic conference for the scientific and engineering innovations of big data.

[4] The 2023 International Conference on Services Computing (SCC 2023, http://thescc.org/) was the flagship theme-topic conference for the services innovation lifecycle that includes enterprise modeling, business consulting, solution creation, services orchestration, services optimization, services management, services marketing, and business process integration and management.

[5] The 2023 International Conference on AI & Mobile Services (AIMS 2023, http://ai1000.org/) was the emerging theme-topic conference for the science and technology of artificial intelligence, and the development, publication, discovery, orchestration, invocation, testing, delivery, and certification of AI-enabled services and mobile applications.

[6] To rapidly respond to the changing economy, the 2023 World Congress on Services (SERVICES 2023, http://metaverse1000.org) was naturally extended to become the International Conference on Metaverse (METAVERSE 2023) to cover immersive services for all vertical industries and area solutions. It put its focus on industry-specific services for digital transformation.

[7] The 2023 International Conference on Cognitive Computing (ICCC 2023, http://thecognitivecomputing.org/) put its focus on the Sensing Intelligence (SI) as a Service (SIaaS) that makes systems listen, speak, see, smell, taste, understand, interact, and walk in the context of scientific research and engineering solutions.

[8] The 2023 International Conference on Internet of Things (ICIOT 2023, http://iciot.org/) put its focus on the creation of Internet of Things technologies and development of IOT services.

[9] The 2023 International Conference on Edge Computing (EDGE 2023, http://theedgecomputing.org/) put its focus on the state of the art and practice of edge computing including but not limited to localized resource sharing, connections with the cloud, and 5G devices and applications.

[10] The 2023 International Conference on Blockchain (ICBC 2023, http://blockchain1000.org/) concentrated on blockchain-based services and enabling technologies.

Some highlights of SCF 2023 are shown below:

– Bigger Platform: The 10 collocated conferences (SCF 2023) were sponsored by the Services Society, which is the world-leading not-for-profit organization (501 c(3)) dedicated to the service of more than 30,000 worldwide Services Computing researchers and practitioners. A bigger platform means bigger opportunities for all volunteers, authors, and participants. Meanwhile, Springer provided sponsorship for best paper awards and other professional activities. All the 10 conference proceedings of SCF 2023 were published by Springer and indexed in the ISI Conference Proceedings Citation Index (included in Web of Science), Engineering Index EI (Compendex and Inspec databases), DBLP, Google Scholar, IO-Port, MathSciNet, Scopus, and zbMATH.

– Brighter Future: While celebrating the 2023 version of ICWS, SCF 2023 highlighted the Second International Conference on Metaverse (METAVERSE 2023), which covered immersive services for all vertical industries and area solutions. Its focus was on industry-specific services for digital transformation. This will lead our community members to create their own brighter future.

– Better Model: SCF 2023 will continue to leverage the invented Conference Blockchain Model (CBM) to innovate the organizing practices for all the 10 theme conferences. Senior researchers in the field are welcome to submit proposals to serve as CBM Ambassador for an individual conference to start better interactions during your leadership role in organizing future SCF conferences.

Contents

Leveraging Blockchain and NFTs for Collaborative Real Estate Transactions

Vinh T. Nguyen$^{(\boxtimes)}$, Triet M. Nguyen$^{(\boxtimes)}$, Hong K. Vo, Khoa T. Dang, Khiem H. Gia, Phuc N. Trong, Bang L. Khanh, and Ngan N. T. Kim

FPT University, Can Tho, Vietnam
vinhntce171035@fpt.edu.vn, trietnm3@fe.edu.vn

Abstract. This paper delves into the transformative potential of block-chain technology and Non-Fungible Tokens (NFTs) in the real estate sector, a critical component of social computing. Traditional real estate transactions are often fraught with inefficiencies, opacity, and a lack of trust, which can hinder the sector's growth and its ability to contribute to social computing. To address these limitations, we introduce a collaborative approach that leverages blockchain technology, smart contracts, NFTs, and the InterPlanetary File System (IPFS). These technologies, when applied to real estate transactions, can enhance transparency, reduce transaction times, and foster a more collaborative and trustful environment. The motivation for this paper is rooted in the need to revolutionize the real estate sector, making it more efficient, transparent, and conducive to social computing. We believe that the integration of blockchain technology and NFTs can significantly contribute to this transformation. Our work makes three significant contributions. First, we propose a novel real estate model based on blockchain technology, which addresses the current limitations in the sector. Second, we implement a proof-of-concept based on the proposed model, demonstrating its feasibility and effectiveness. Lastly, we deploy the proof-of-concept on four EVM-supported platforms, namely BNB Smart Chain, Fantom, Polygon, and Celo. This allows us to evaluate each platform's suitability for our proposed model, ensuring optimal performance and efficiency.

Keywords: Real estate · Blockchain · Smart contracts · NFT · IPFS · Ethereum · Fantom · Polygon · Binance Smart Chain

1 Introduction

The real estate sector is a significant contributor to the economic stability and growth of a country. As reported by Eurostat in 2015, the real estate activities sector alone accounted for 1.9% of the total workforce and 5.6% of the total number of enterprises in the European Union [3]. Beyond its economic impact, real estate also influences social computing, shaping the dynamics of urban development, community interactions, and socio-economic structures. However, the

© The Author(s), under exclusive license to Springer Nature Switzerland AG 2024
M. Luo and L.-J. Zhang (Eds.): CLOUD 2023, LNCS 14204, pp. 1–14, 2024.
https://doi.org/10.1007/978-3-031-51709-9_1

traditional approach to real estate transactions is fraught with limitations. High brokerage fees, lack of transparency, time-consuming processes, and susceptibility to fraud are just a few of the challenges plaguing the sector [6,11].

In recent years, collaborative technologies such as blockchain and smart contracts have emerged as potential solutions to these problems [7,8]. Blockchain technology, with its decentralized, immutable, and transparent nature, can revolutionize the way tangible and intangible assets are transferred and recorded [23]. Smart contracts, which are self-executing contracts with the terms of the agreement directly written into code, can establish technical obligations, thereby preventing parties from violating their obligations [13]. These technologies can enhance trust among stakeholders, reduce the time required for negotiation and due diligence processes, and promote the reliability of information [26].

Several initiatives have been launched worldwide to apply blockchain, smart contracts, and Non-Fungible Tokens (NFTs) to address the traditional problems of real estate transactions. For instance, Sweden's land registry, Lantmäteriet, launched a pilot project to evaluate potential blockchain applications for real estate transactions, which is predicted to save about 100 million euros [6,11]. Similarly, in the Netherlands, the government has initiated several blockchain pilots with real estate, introducing the concept of Crowd Ownership [6]. However, these approaches are not without their limitations. They often require significant changes to existing legal frameworks, and the tokenization of real estate assets can create challenges related to governance and liquidity [2,5,9].

This paper, "Leveraging Blockchain and NFTs for Collaborative Real Estate Transactions", aims to address these limitations by proposing a novel blockchain-based real estate system. Our proposed system leverages the power of blockchain technology, smart contracts, and NFTs to increase the liquidity of the real estate asset market, enhance security, and make real estate investments more attractive [24,25]. It addresses the lack of transparency in the peer-to-peer economy, reduces high brokerage or intermediary fees, and streamlines the process of real estate transactions [6].

Our proposed blockchain-based model for real estate transactions has three main contributions. First, it proposes a model of the Real Estate Sector based on Collaborative Technology (i.e., Blockchain, Smart contract, and NFT) with all the information logged in the InterPlanetary File System (IPFS). This approach ensures the immutability and transparency of real estate data. Second, it implements and publicizes the proposed model as a proof-of-concept on the Ethereum platform using smart contracts written in the Solidity language. This implementation demonstrates the practical feasibility of our model. Finally, it evaluates the proposed model by deploying our implementation on four Ethereum Virtual Machine (EVM)-supported platforms, namely BNB Smart Chain, Fantom, Polygon, and Celo. This multi-platform deployment allows for a comprehensive evaluation of our model's performance and scalability.

2   Related Work

The application of blockchain technology and Non-Fungible Tokens (NFTs) in real estate transactions has been a subject of interest in various studies. This section presents a review of related works, focusing on the use of blockchain and NFTs in real estate transactions across different countries and the potential benefits and challenges associated with their implementation.

In Sweden, Lantmäteriet, the country's land registry, initiated a pilot project in 2016 to explore the potential of blockchain for real estate transactions [10]. The project aimed to streamline the contracting process and was predicted to save about 100 million euros [11]. The project has since moved to the implementation stage, with the technology being used for land and real estate registration on a small scale using a private blockchain.

In the Netherlands, several blockchain pilots have been launched at the national level, including open data from cadastral and a government-wide pilot of the capabilities of the processes [6]. In Brazil, a blockchain pilot project was launched in 2017 by the real estate registry office, Cartório de Registro de Imóveis, in partnership with blockchain technology company Ubitquity, with the aim of improving the accuracy, confidentiality, and transparency of the land registration process [6,22].

In the Republic of Georgia, Bitfury Corporation and the National Public Registry (NAPR) developed a blockchain-based land tenure system, an experimental project that aimed to migrate the nation's land registry system to a blockchain platform [6]. In the United States, REX, founded in 2016, promises a new diversified listing system (MLS) standard for real estate brokers [5].

In Ukraine, Bitfury and the State Agency of E-Government of Ukraine signed a memorandum of understanding in 2017 on the transfer of land cadastral of Ukraine to blockchain [4]. In Japan, the government is developing projects that use blockchain technology to register assets, manage and unify all procedures related to assets [10].

Several studies have also discussed the concept of asset tokenization, where real-world assets are digitally represented and recorded on an immutable decentralized ledger [1,24,25]. This concept has been applied to real estate, where ownership can be converted into a digital token backed by the asset itself, increasing the liquidity of the real estate asset market and making real estate investments more attractive [24].

Despite the potential benefits of blockchain and NFTs in real estate transactions, several challenges exist. These include lack of transparency in the peer-to-peer economy, high brokerage or intermediary fees, fake reviews and descriptions of the property and its quality, and time-consuming processes [6]. However, it is argued that blockchain technology has the potential to address most of these problems and achieve decentralization of the process of real estate transportation and land registration [11].

In conclusion, the related works highlight the potential of blockchain technology and NFTs in revolutionizing real estate transactions. However, more research is needed to address the challenges associated with their implementation and to fully realize their potential in this domain.

3   Approach

In this section, we present traditional real estate management models before proposing an approach based on Blockchain technology, smart contracts, and NFT.

3.1   Traditional Real Estate Management Model

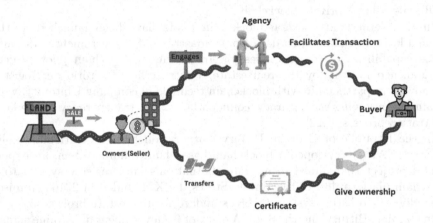

Fig. 1. Traditional real estate management model

There are commonly five components in the traditional model[1], namely:

- **Land (L)**: This is the property that is being bought or sold. It's the fundamental component of any real estate transaction.
- **Certificate (C)**: This is the legal document that proves ownership of the land. It's typically issued by a government agency.
- **Owners/Seller (O)**: The current owner of the land who wants to sell it.
- **Buyer (B)**: The person or entity that wants to buy the land.
- **Agency (A)**: This is the real estate agency that facilitates the transaction between the buyer and the seller. They handle the logistics of the sale and ensure all legal requirements are met.

Figure 1 shows the traditional approach for the real estate management[2]. In particular, **(L)** - This is the property that is being bought or sold. It's the

---

[1] We provide the traditional model for the sale activities. For the rent activities, the model is designed in the same idea.

[2] Each arrow in the model represents a relationship or action between the components of the model. For example, the **(O)** engage the Agency to facilitate the transaction, and they transfer the Certificate to the Buyer to give them ownership of the Land.

fundamental component of any real estate transaction. (**O**) - The current owner of the land who wants to sell it. They engage a real estate agency to facilitate the transaction. (**A**) - This is the real estate agency that facilitates the transaction between the buyer and the seller. They handle the logistics of the sale and ensure all legal requirements are met. (**B**) - The person or entity that wants to buy the land. They work with the agency to complete the transaction. (**C**) - This is the legal document that proves ownership of the land. It's typically issued by a government agency. The seller transfers the certificate to the buyer, giving them ownership of the land.

3.2   Real Estate Management Model Based on Blockchain Technology, Smart Contract, and NFT

Based on the proposed model, we define three new component which present in Fig. 2, namely IPFS; Blockchain & Smart Contract; and NFT. We also remove the role of Certificate (C) in the upgrade version. The role of the three extra components is presented below:

- **NFT**: NFTs can represent ownership of a unique piece of property on the blockchain. This can provide a secure and transparent way to prove ownership of property.
- **Blockchain & Smart Contract (BC)**: These technologies can provide a transparent and immutable record of all transactions, helping to build trust and prevent fraud. Smart contracts can automate many of the processes involved in real estate transactions, making them faster and more efficient.
- **InterPlanetary File System (IPFS)**: IPFS can be used to store data in a decentralized way, reducing reliance on centralized servers. This can increase the resilience and reliability of the system.

In the upgrade version, (**L**) is the property that is being bought or sold. It's the fundamental component of any real estate transaction. (**O**) wants to sell it. They engage a real estate agency to facilitate the transaction. (**A**) facilitates the transaction between the buyer and the seller. They handle the logistics of the sale and ensure all legal requirements are met. (**B**) wants to buy the land. They work with the agency to complete the transaction. **NFT** represents ownership of the land. The seller transfers the NFT to the buyer, giving them ownership of the land. (**BC**) records the transaction on the blockchain, providing a transparent and immutable record. The smart contract automates the transaction process, making it faster and more efficient. IPFS stores data in a decentralized way, reducing reliance on centralized servers and increasing the resilience and reliability of the system.

We propose the workflow of the real estate management model in Fig. 3. Firstly, the process begins when the current owners of the land, who want to sell it, engage a real estate agency. The agency then facilitates the transaction between the buyer and the seller, handling the logistics of the sale and ensuring all legal requirements are met. Simultaneously, the seller transfers a

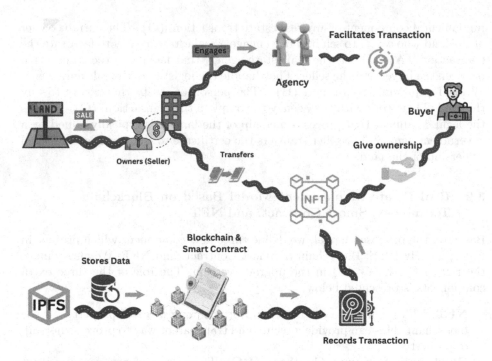

Fig. 2. Real estate management model based on blockchain technology, smart contract, and NFT

Non-Fungible Token (NFT) that represents ownership of the land to the buyer, effectively giving them ownership. This transaction is recorded on the blockchain through smart contract technology, providing a transparent and immutable record. The smart contract also automates the transaction process, making it faster and more efficient. Finally, the InterPlanetary File System (IPFS) stores the data related to the transaction in a decentralized way. This reduces reliance on centralized servers and increases the resilience and reliability of the system.

This model leverages the power of blockchain technology, NFTs, and IPFS to address the limitations of traditional real estate models, providing a more transparent, efficient, and accessible solution.

4   Evaluation Scenarios

4.1   Evaluation Setting

We have previously evaluated system responsiveness, including the number of successful and failed requests and system latency (minimum, maximum, and average), in our prior research. In this paper, we extend our evaluation to determine the most suitable platform for our proposed model. Instead of defining security policies such as access control, we implement our proposed model on Ethereum Virtual Machine (EVM)-enabled blockchain platforms. This approach

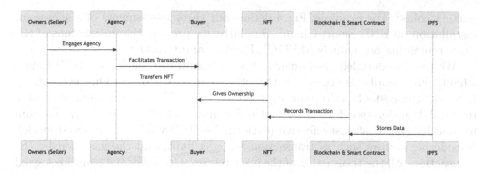

Fig. 3. The workflow of the real estate management model

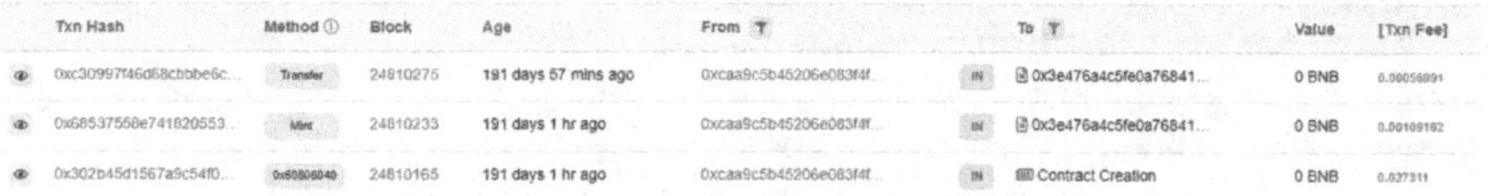

Fig. 4. The transaction info (e.g., BNB Smart Chain)

Fig. 5. NFT creation   **Fig. 6.** NFT transfer

allows us to leverage existing platforms and systems, thereby broadening the reach and applicability of our model.

In particular, we propose an innovative model that harnesses the capabilities of blockchain technology and Non-Fungible Tokens (NFTs) to transform the real estate sector. This model is designed to address the limitations of current real estate approaches and to enhance the efficiency and transparency of real estate transactions. In practice, we deploy our model on four popular EVM-supported blockchain platforms: Binance Smart Chain (BNB Smart Chain)[3], Polygon[4], Fantom[5], and Celo[6].

Our implementations on these platforms serve as a contribution to the field, providing insights into the transaction fees associated with each platform's sup-

---

[3] https://github.com/bnb-chain/whitepaper/blob/master/WHITEPAPER.md.
[4] https://polygon.technology/lightpaper-polygon.pdf.
[5] https://whitepaper.io/document/438/fantom-whitepaper.
[6] https://celo.org/papers/whitepaper.

porting coins[7]. For example, Fig. 4 details our three assessments of a successful installation on BNB Smart Chain[8]. Similarly, we prepare the initial steps of the three remaining on, namely MATIC[9], FTM[10], and CELO[11].

We provide detailed assessments of a successful installation on BNB Smart Chain, with similar settings for the other three platforms. Our evaluations focus on the cost of performing contract creation, NFT generation, and NFT retrieval/transfer (see Figs. 4, 5, and 6 for more detail), respectively. We aim to identify the most cost-effective platform for deploying our proposed model, considering factors such as transaction fee, gas limit, and the gas used by the transaction. All the transaction of the NFT retrieval/transfer (i.e., land) is logged on the main chain (e.g., Fig. 7 presents the 5 contract events)

Fig. 7. The latest five contracts events (e.g., BNB Smart Chain)

Through this comprehensive evaluation, we aim to provide a robust and efficient solution for leveraging blockchain and NFTs for collaborative real estate transactions.

---

[7] We have provide the source code of our proof-of-concepts of blockchain-based real estate management system in https://github.com/SonHaXuan/real_estate.

[8] https://testnet.bscscan.com/address/0x3e476a4c5fe0a7684125d077f7ccb385610ce ec3.

[9] https://mumbai.polygonscan.com/address/0x3e476a4c5fe0a7684125d077f7ccb38561 0ceec3.

[10] https://testnet.ftmscan.com/address/0x3e476a4c5fe0a7684125d077f7ccb385610ce ec3.

[11] https://explorer.celo.org/alfajores/address/0x3E476a4C5Fe0A7684125D077f7CCb3 85610CEeC3/transactions.

4.2   Transaction Fee

Table 1 provides a comprehensive overview of the transaction fees for each operation on the respective platforms. The fees are denoted in the native cryptocurrency of each platform, along with their equivalent value in US dollars for easy comparison.

Table 1. Transaction fee

	Contract Creation	Create NFT	Transfer NFT
BNB Smart Chain	0.027311 BNB ($8.33)	0.00109162 BNB ($0.33)	0.00056991 BNB ($0.17)
Fantom	0.0095767 FTM ($0.003)	0.000405167 FTM ($0.000127)	0.0002380105 FTM ($0.000075)
Polygon	0.0068405000328344 MATIC ($0.01)	0.000289405001273382 MATIC ($0.00)	0.000170007500748033 MATIC ($0.00)
Celo	0.00709722 CELO ($0.004)	0.0002840812 CELO ($0.000)	0.0001554878 CELO ($0.000)

As can be seen from the table, there is a significant variation in transaction costs across the platforms. For instance, BNB Smart Chain incurs the highest transaction fee for contract creation, amounting to $8.33, while the other platforms charge less than a cent for the same operation. The costs for creating and transferring NFTs also exhibit substantial differences across the platforms.

This detailed comparison provides valuable insights for blockchain experts and developers in choosing the most cost-effective platform for deploying blockchain-based solutions, particularly in the context of real estate transactions. The choice of platform can significantly impact the overall cost-effectiveness and scalability of the solution, making this analysis crucial for informed decision-making.

4.3   Gas Limit

Table 2 presents the gas limit for three key operations: Contract Creation, NFT (Non-Fungible Token) Creation, and NFT Transfer, across the four platforms.

Table 2. Gas limit

	Contract Creation	Create NFT	Transfer NFT
BNB Smart Chain	2,731,100	109,162	71,991
Fantom	2,736,200	115,762	72,803
Polygon	2,736,476	115,762	72,803
Celo	3,548,610	142,040	85,673

As shown in the table, the gas limit varies across the platforms and operations. For instance, BNB Smart Chain has a gas limit of 2,731,100 for contract creation, while Celo has a significantly higher gas limit of 3,548,610 for the same operation. Similarly, the gas limit for creating and transferring NFTs also differs across the platforms.

This analysis is crucial for blockchain developers and experts, as the gas limit directly impacts the complexity and size of the operations that can be performed on the blockchain. A higher gas limit allows for more complex operations, but it also increases the computational resources required for processing the operations. Therefore, understanding the gas limit is essential for optimizing the performance and cost-effectiveness of blockchain-based solutions, particularly in the context of real estate transactions.

4.4   Gas Used by Transaction

Table 3 presents the gas used by three key operations: Contract Creation, NFT (Non-Fungible Token) Creation, and NFT Transfer, across the four platforms. The values are also expressed as a percentage of the Gas Used by Transaction for each operation, providing a measure of the efficiency of the transaction.

Table 3. Gas Used by Transaction

	Contract Creation	Create NFT	Transfer NFT
BNB Smart Chain	2,731,340 (100%)	109,162 (100%)	56,991 (79.16%)
Fantom	2,736,200 (100%)	115,762 (100%)	68,003 (93.41%)
Polygon	2,736,284 (100%)	115,762 (100%)	68,003 (93.41%)
Celo	2,736,200 (76.92%)	109,262 (76.92%)	59,803 (69.8%)

As shown in the table, the gas used by each operation varies across the platforms. For instance, BNB Smart Chain uses 100% of the gas limit for contract creation and NFT creation, while only 79.16% of the gas limit is used for NFT transfer. On the other hand, Celo uses only 76.92% of the gas limit for contract creation and NFT creation, and 69.8% for NFT transfer.

This analysis is crucial for blockchain developers and experts, as the gas used by a transaction directly impacts the cost and efficiency of the operations on the blockchain. A lower percentage of gas used indicates a more efficient transaction, reducing the overall cost. Therefore, understanding the gas used by each transaction is essential for optimizing the performance and cost-effectiveness of blockchain-based solutions, in the context of real estate transactions.

5   Discussion

5.1   Threats to Validity

While our study provides valuable insights into the use of blockchain and NFTs for collaborative real estate transactions, there are several threats to validity that should be considered.

Firstly, our evaluation was conducted on four specific EVM-compatible blockchain platforms: Binance Smart Chain (BNB), Fantom, Polygon, and Celo. While these platforms are widely used and representative of the current blockchain landscape, the results may not generalize to other blockchain platforms, particularly those that do not support EVM.

Secondly, the cost of transactions in terms of transaction fees, gas limit, and gas used by transaction can vary over time due to factors such as network congestion, changes in the price of the native cryptocurrency, and updates to the blockchain protocols. Therefore, the costs reported in this study represent a snapshot at the time of the evaluation and may not reflect the costs at other times.

Lastly, the efficiency and cost-effectiveness of the operations on the blockchain can be influenced by the specific implementation of the smart contracts and the complexity of the real estate transactions. In this study, we used a standard implementation and relatively simple transactions. More complex transactions could require more computational resources and thus result in higher costs.

5.2   Our Findings

Our evaluation of the four EVM-compatible blockchain platforms revealed significant differences in the cost and efficiency of real estate transactions implemented using blockchain and NFTs.

In terms of transaction fees, BNB Smart Chain had the highest costs, while Fantom and Celo had the lowest costs. This suggests that the choice of blockchain platform can have a significant impact on the cost of real estate transactions.

In terms of gas limit and gas used by transaction, all four platforms were relatively similar, with BNB Smart Chain and Polygon being slightly more efficient than Fantom and Celo. This indicates that the computational complexity of the transactions is relatively consistent across the platforms.

Overall, our findings suggest that while all four platforms can support collaborative real estate transactions using blockchain and NFTs, there are trade-offs in terms of cost and efficiency that need to be considered.

5.3   Future Work

Our study opens several avenues for future research. We proceed to implement more complex methods/algorithms (i.e., encryption and decryption) as well as more complex data structures to observe the costs for the respective transactions. Deploying the proposed model in a real environment is also a possible approach (i.e., implementing the recommendation system on the FTM mainnet). In our current analysis, we have not considered issues related to the privacy policy of users (i.e., access control [14,16], dynamic policy [15,27]) - a possible approach would be implemented in upcoming research activities. Secondly, future work could investigate the impact of different implementations of the smart contracts and the complexity of the real estate transactions on the cost and efficiency of the operations on the blockchain. This could provide insights into how to optimize the implementation of real estate transactions on the blockchain.

Thirdly, future research could explore the use of other blockchain technologies, such as decentralized finance (DeFi) and decentralized autonomous organizations (DAOs), in the context of real estate transactions. This could open up new possibilities for collaborative real estate transactions and further enhance the efficiency and transparency of the real estate market. Finally, infrastructure-based approaches (i.e., gRPC [12,19]; Microservices [17,20]; Dynamic transmission messages [21] and Brokerless [18]) can be integrated into the model of us to increase user interaction (i.e., API-call-based approach).

6   Conclusion

In this paper, we have explored the potential of blockchain technology and Non-Fungible Tokens (NFTs) to revolutionize real estate transactions within the context of social computing. The current real estate transaction systems often face challenges related to transparency, efficiency, and security, which can be significantly improved by leveraging the collaborative nature of blockchain and the unique properties of NFTs. Our proposed model provides a decentralized, transparent, and secure platform for real estate transactions, fostering collaboration and trust among participants. This aligns with the principles of social computing, where technology is used to facilitate and enhance social interactions. We have implemented a proof-of-concept based on this model and deployed it on four Ethereum Virtual Machine (EVM)-supported platforms, namely Binance Smart Chain (BNB), Fantom, Polygon, and Celo. Our evaluations focused on transaction fees, gas limits, and gas used by transactions, providing valuable insights into the performance and cost-effectiveness of each platform.

Our findings suggest that blockchain and NFTs can significantly enhance the social computing aspects of real estate transactions. The use of smart contracts ensures the enforcement of transaction rules, while NFTs provide a unique representation of property ownership. Furthermore, the use of IPFS ensures the persistence and accessibility of transaction data, promoting transparency and trust among participants. However, our work is not without limitations. The validity of our findings is subject to the performance of the selected EVM-supported platforms and the specific implementation of our proof-of-concept. Future work will focus on addressing these limitations and further refining our model.

In general, our work contributes to the ongoing discourse on the application of blockchain technology and NFTs in real estate within the realm of social computing. We believe that our proposed model and findings provide a solid foundation for future research and practical applications in this area. We hope that our work will inspire further innovations in leveraging blockchain and NFTs for collaborative real estate transactions, fostering a more collaborative and transparent real estate sector.

References

1. Avantaggiato, M., Gallo, P.: Challenges and opportunities using multichain for real estate. In: 2019 IEEE International Black Sea Conference on Communications and Networking (BlackSeaCom) (2019)
2. Deloitte: Blockchain and smart contracts could transform property transactions. Wall Street J., January 2018. http://deloitte.wsj.com/cfo/2018/01/03/blockchain-and-smart-contracts-could-transform-property-transactions/
3. EUROSTAT: Real estate activity statistics - NACE Rev. 2. (2015). https://ec.europa.eu/eurostat/statistics-explained/index.php?title=Real_estate_activity_statistics_-_NACE_Rev._2&oldid=572702
4. Kalyuzhnova, N.: Transformation of the real estate market on the basis of use of the blockchain technologies: opportunities and problems. In: MATEC Web of Conferences 212 (2018)
5. Konashevych, O.: Constraints and benefits of the blockchain use for real estate and property rights. J. Property Plan. Environ. Law **12**(2), 109–127 (2020)
6. Krupa, K.S.J., Akhil, M.S.: Reshaping the real estate industry using blockchain. In: Sridhar, V., Padma, M.C., Rao, K.A.R. (eds.) Emerging Research in Electronics, Computer Science and Technology. LNEE, vol. 545, pp. 255–263. Springer, Singapore (2019). https://doi.org/10.1007/978-981-13-5802-9_24
7. Le, H.T., et al.: Introducing multi shippers mechanism for decentralized cash on delivery system. Int. J. Adv. Comput. Sci. Appl. **10**(6), 591–597 (2019)
8. Le, N.T.T., et al.: Assuring non-fraudulent transactions in cash on delivery by introducing double smart contracts. Int. J. Adv. Comput. Sci. Appl. **10**(5), 677–684 (2019)
9. McKeon, S.: Traditional asset tokenization. Hackernoon, August 2017. https://hackernoon.com/traditional-asset-tokenization-b8a59585a7e0
10. Mezquita, Y., Parra, J., Perez, E., Prieto, J., Corchado, J.M.: Blockchain-based systems in land registry, a survey of their use and economic implications. In: Herrero, Á., Cambra, C., Urda, D., Sedano, J., Quintián, H., Corchado, E. (eds.) CISIS 2019. AISC, vol. 1267, pp. 13–22. Springer, Cham (2021). https://doi.org/10.1007/978-3-030-57805-3_2
11. Nasarre-Aznar, S.: Collaborative housing and blockchain. Administration **66**(2), 59–82 (2018)
12. Nguyen, L.T.T., et al.: BMDD: a novel approach for IoT platform (broker-less and microservice architecture, decentralized identity, and dynamic transmission messages). PeerJ Comput. Sci. **8**, e950 (2022)
13. Savelyev, A.: Contract law 2.0: 'smart' contracts as the beginning of the end of classic contract law. Inf. Commun. Technol. Law **26**(2), 116–134 (2017)
14. Son, H.X., Hoang, N.M.: A novel attribute-based access control system for fine-grained privacy protection. In: Proceedings of the 3rd International Conference on Cryptography, Security and Privacy, pp. 76–80 (2019)
15. Son, H.X., Dang, T.K., Massacci, F.: REW-SMT: a new approach for rewriting XACML request with dynamic big data security policies. In: Wang, G., Atiquzzaman, M., Yan, Z., Choo, K.-K.R. (eds.) SpaCCS 2017. LNCS, vol. 10656, pp. 501–515. Springer, Cham (2017). https://doi.org/10.1007/978-3-319-72389-1_40
16. Son, H.X., Nguyen, M.H., Vo, H.K., Nguyen, T.P.: Toward an privacy protection based on access control model in hybrid cloud for healthcare systems. In: Martínez Álvarez, F., Troncoso Lora, A., Sáez Muñoz, J.A., Quintián, H., Corchado, E. (eds.) CISIS/ICEUTE -2019. AISC, vol. 951, pp. 77–86. Springer, Cham (2020). https://doi.org/10.1007/978-3-030-20005-3_8

17. Thanh, L.N.T., et al.: IoHT-MBA: an internet of healthcare things (IoHT) platform based on microservice and brokerless architecture. Int. J. Adv. Comput. Sci. Appli. **12**(7), 594–601 (2021)
18. Thanh, L.N.T., et al.: SIP-MBA: a secure IoT platform with brokerless and microservice architecture. Int. J. Adv. Comput. Sci. Appli. **12**, 586–593 (2021)
19. Thanh, L.N.T., et al.: Toward a security IoT platform with high rate transmission and low energy consumption. In: Gervasi, O., et al. (eds.) ICCSA 2021. LNCS, vol. 12949, pp. 647–662. Springer, Cham (2021). https://doi.org/10.1007/978-3-030-86653-2_47
20. Nguyen, T.T.L., et al.: Toward a unique IoT network via single sign-on protocol and message queue. In: Saeed, K., Dvorský, J. (eds.) CISIM 2021. LNCS, vol. 12883, pp. 270–284. Springer, Cham (2021). https://doi.org/10.1007/978-3-030-84340-3_22
21. Thanh, L.N.T., et al.: UIP2SOP: a unique IoT network applying single sign-on and message queue protocol. IJACSA **12**(6), 19–30 (2021)
22. Ubitquity: Ubitquity® the enterprise-ready blockchain-secured platform for real estate recordkeeping. https://www.ubitquity.io
23. Veuger, J.: Trust in a viable real estate economy with disruption and blockchain. Facilities **36**, 103–120 (2018)
24. Vidal, M.T.: Tokenizing real estate on the blockchain. Medium, July 2017. https://medium.com/@mariat.vidal/tokenizing-real-estate-on-the-blockchain-9a13ae99bf11
25. Wolfson, R.: The future of investing: tokenizing traditional assets on the blockchain. HuffPost, November 2017. https://www.huffingtonpost.com/entry/the-future-of-investing-tokenizing-traditional-assets_us_5a0f4aaee4b023121e0e927d
26. Wouda, H.P., Opdenakker, R.: Blockchain technology in commercial real estate transactions. J. Prop. Invest. Financ. **37**, 570–579 (2019)
27. Xuan, S.H., et al.: Rew-XAC: an approach to rewriting request for elastic ABAC enforcement with dynamic policies. In: 2016 International Conference on Advanced Computing and Applications (ACOMP), pp. 25–31. IEEE (2016)

Dialectical Relationship Analysis of Data Governance Elements in the Financial Format—Based on the "Voyage Chart" Architecture

Shiming Shen[1,3(✉)] and Jing Lu[2]

[1] Shanghai University of Finance and Economics, No. 777 Guoding Road, Yangpu District, Shanghai 200433, P.R. China
simonshen@live.com
[2] University of Alberta, 116 St and 85 Ave, Edmonton, AB T6G 2R3, Canada
[3] DAMA China, 2 76-78 Jiangchang San Lu, Suite 806, Jingan District, Shanghai, China

Abstract. Although the economic value of data has received widespread attention, most financial enterprises still have differences in cognition of digital transformation compared with the banking industry, which has always focused on the accumulation of digital capabilities, especially in the understanding and practice of data management systems. Aiming at the topic of how to promote data management capacity building based on the existing digital foundation of enterprises, the author draws a "data governance voyage chart" based on the relevant theory of DMBOK 2.0 and the research of the financial leasing industry, aiming to analyze the dynamic balance theory between the elements of data governance by discussing the dialectical relationship between the five elements of "wind", "tower", "ship", "sail" and "sea", and share relevant thoughts on deepening data governance in the financial industry.

Keywords: Data governance · Financial leasing · Digital transformation

1 Data Governance Element "Voyage Chart": Based on the Financial Leasing Industry

According to the DAMA's theory, data governance refers to the "process of management and optimization around the data life cycle" [1], and in the book DMBOK 2.0 compiled and published by the association, the dependence between people, processes and technologies is revealed through the hexagonal diagram of environmental factors, which is significant in revealing the guiding significance of goals and principles for data governance activities, and also provides a theoretical framework for how to describe the chapters of the data management (Fig. 1).

Fig. 1. Hexagonal diagram of environmental factors (Source: DAMA-DMBOK 2.0)

When practicing enterprise data governance, although the seventeen chapters in the book have provided a large number of tools and processes to guide practitioners to practice data governance, it seems that it is still very difficult to establish an effective data governance system from 0 to 1 in the face of complex internal and external environments of enterprises. Given the differences between industries and enterprises, it is often difficult for data governance practitioners to quickly locate data governance goals and meet expectations within a specific time frame, which is one of the reasons why while most enterprises are shouting about digital transformation and valuing the value of data, only a few have achieved success in data management.

In the past, as far as the author's financial leasing industry is concerned, the requirements for digital capacity building of traditional businesses were not high, and the necessary conditions for most business development were the due diligence results of business personnel and the reports formed after comprehensive analysis of industries and enterprises, coupled with the relatively small pressure of financial supervision in the past, the foundation of digital construction was relatively weak compared with the banking and insurance industries in the absence of driving force, and generally failed to precipitate data assets well.

In recent years, there are two main factors that have accelerated the digital capacity building of the financial leasing industry, the first is the macro background of digital transformation. In 2015, China's State Council issued "Made in China 2025", which first provided directional guidance for promoting the transformation of the manufacturing industry to digitalization and intelligence, and then issued the "New Generation Artificial Intelligence Development Plan", "New Generation Information Technology Development Strategy", "Notice on Accelerating the Digital Transformation of State-owned Enterprises" and other documents, gradually leading relevant enterprises to accelerate digital capacity building [2]. Secondly, the regulatory compliance pressure brought about by the financial leasing industry after the regulatory functions were clearly assigned to the Financial Services Bureau has also prompted enterprises to generate endogenous momentum. After 2018, the regulatory functions of financial leasing companies were clearly assigned to the CBIRC (now known as the State Financial Regulatory Administration), and then "the Interim Measures for the Supervision and Administration of Financial Leasing Companies "promulgated in 2020 clearly stated that the CBIRC was responsible for the overall formulation of management rules, which put forward clearer regulatory requirements for financial leasing companies, in which data was used as an important carrier of financial supervision [3], which upgraded digital capacity building from "multiple choice questions" to "mandatory questions".

Driven by digital transformation and regulatory pressure, financial leasing companies have accelerated the construction of digital capabilities, resulting in a large amount of data and information (which cannot be called assets at this time), so how to establish good data management capabilities has become the next major issue facing most financial leasing companies. After visiting and understanding the financial leasing industry, the author believes that the main problems faced by enterprises in the financial industry are mainly the conflict between the identification of long-term goals and the unclear short-term path, coupled with the current concepts of "data middle platform", "data elements", "data transactions" and "data compliance" that have been repeatedly mentioned and interpreted by all parties, but have added trouble to the unknown governance road that enterprises have not yet set foot on (Fig. 2).

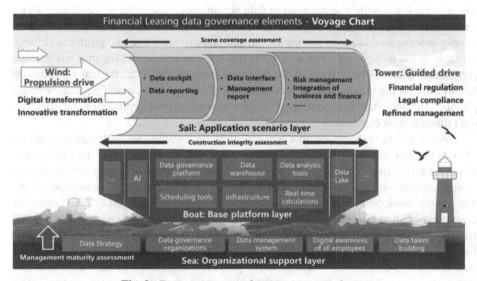

Fig. 2. Data governance elements - voyage chart

Based on the observation and thinking of the above situation, in order to clearly describe the dialectical relationship between the elements of data governance, after referring to the "DAMA-DMBOK 2.0", "the strategy in data of Huawei" [4], "Data Governance: Strategies, Methods, Tools an Practice" [5] and other literature materials, the author combined with the actual situation summarized after the investigation and visit of various financial leasing companies to draw the "Financial Leasing data governance elements - voyage chart", which displays the elements that constitute data governance in a graphical way, from "wind", "tower", "ship", "sail" and "sea" From the perspective of the five elements, it briefly describes how to establish enterprise-level data governance capabilities from 0 to 1, and analyzes the possible problems in the data governance process in order to deepen the topic.

2 Analyze the Dialectical Development Relationship Between Elements

Based on the understanding and induction of DMBOK 2.0, this paper will refines the data governance elements into four items, namely driving force, application scenario, support platform and organizational guarantee, of which the driving force is divided into two categories: guidance and promotion, a total of five elements. In order to better understand the relationship between the five elements of data governance, the following will be based on the deconstruction of this voyage chart to understand the dialectical development relationship between the analysis elements.

2.1 Driving Force Elements: "Wind" and "Tower"

The driving force is the starting point of data governance, first, without the driving force can not even talk about digitalization, in the financial format of the driving force can be simply summarized into two categories: propulsion driving force and guidance driving force, here the author compares it to the two necessary conditions for ship navigation: power and goal. As mentioned in the previous chapter, the financial leasing industry is currently facing the dual challenges of business transformation and regulatory compliance. Turning challenges into opportunities requires digital approaches and effective data management capabilities.

"Wind" refers to the power, that is, why enterprises want to actively manage data, in view of the special format of financial leasing, its upstream connection to the capital end, downstream connection to the asset end. In the context of digital economy and intelligent manufacturing, the upstream and downstream ecology of financial leasing enterprises are vigorously developing digital capabilities [6], and the end will be used as a medium with data to establish a connection, which is one of the main driving forces of financial leasing transformation: through the establishment of a good data management system to carry the data resources generated upstream and downstream. Using data assets to identify new business opportunities, or using data to provide competitive services upstream and downstream to enhance its position in the value chain, is collectively referred to as the driving force for improving data management capabilities.

And "tower" refers to the goal, direction, that is, data management capabilities should develop in what direction, in practice the author roughly summarizes the guidance driving force of the financial format into regulatory requirements, compliance requirements, management requirements three directions, the difference between the guiding driving force and the driving force is that the guiding type does not transfer the will within the organization, but according to the expectations of the upper management body after decomposition in the form of policies, norms, requirements and other forms of concrete embodiment, For example, the guiding driving force in the current financial leasing industry is reflected in the specific requirements for data put forward by the submission supervision [7], the relevant regulations on data security, and the corporate responsibility of listed companies in ESG governance, which jointly guide the development direction of data governance in the financial leasing industry, so they are collectively referred to as the guiding driving force.

2.2 Application Scenario Elements: "Sail"

After clarifying the two drivers mentioned above, the next action for companies is to decompose: implement the goal or motivation into specific scenarios that need to be applied to data, so the sail is likened to a scene symbol that carries the "driving force". When enterprises practice the data governance capability system, they should first decompose the driving force goals into application scenarios according to the principle of importance, and the clarification of the scenarios will help evaluate the success of the data governance system. In addition, with the strengthening of current financial supervision, compliance management [8] and risk control [9] have gradually become one of the important scenarios for data application. It should be noted that the "sail" is dynamically changing, and when the core application scenarios are satisfied, with the gradual enrichment of data resources, enterprises will put forward more demands based on application scenarios, and for this reason, how to match the elements discussed in this article for dynamic development is particularly important.

2.3 Basic Platform Elements: "Ship"

The basic platform mainly refers to the technical means and implementation results to support the realization of application scenarios, although the main focus of suppliers in the current data industry is concentrated here, but perhaps it is more important to think clearly about "wind" and "sail" before carrying out "construction. In today's information explosion, "data middle platform", "lake warehouse integration", "big data" and other terms have long been strange, the author believes that the entire industry objectively has the problem of excessive consumption, most enterprises have not yet formed basic capabilities but in the concept has been first transported by various stakeholders a wave of too advanced concepts, resulting in the capacity building cycle and expectations of the matching of too irrational expectations, if not pay attention to the correction of the goal is prone to the phenomenon of bad money driving out good money, and then lead to the implementation of the project repeatedly, A vicious circle that consumes the costs of enterprises for a long time.

Under the premise that the current technical capabilities can better guarantee the application scenarios, it is necessary to properly plan the medium-term future based on the needs of the application scenarios, and properly plan the mid-term future after the guarantee goals are clear, so as to ensure that the "hull" and "sail" dimensions match as much as possible, and avoid the situation that the sail is too large and the sampan is too small. However, it is undeniable that the "hull" (platform realization) must be initially designed with future scalability in mind, and while achieving the initial goals, it is possible to gradually expand the real-time computing, AI, big data computing and other future innovation capabilities of the "hull" in a modular componentized manner.

2.4 Organizational Support Elements: "Sea"

"Ocean" is the environment that carries sailboats, in terms of conventional logic of navigation, the depth of the ocean should match the weight of the entire sailing ship to be loaded, if the 10,000-ton ship is sailing in a small river then there is a risk of running aground, similarly,a little ship is difficult to sail too far in the sea. In this article, "ocean" refers to the organizational culture guarantee of enterprises, which also corresponds to the chapters of data management organization, change management, and data culture in DMBOK 2.0. As the continuous voyage advances, the level of organizational security should be deepened simultaneously, and managers should lay out the establishment of employees data strategy and organizational culture in advance [10]. In particular, it should be noted that the construction of this element is a long-term and slow process, and it is not appropriate to forcibly promote the establishment of data for employees culture within the organization without clear goals and appropriate landing platform to support it, because it is often difficult for enterprises to realize the importance of this element at this time, and it is easy to float on the surface and difficult to promote deeply.

3   The Root Cause of Most Enterprise Data Management Failures: Element Imbalance

Chairman Wang of DAMA China and many other experts have written and shared their own experience about the common reasons for enterprise data governance failure [11], mainly including lack of goals, unclear rights and responsibilities, insufficient high-level attention, lack of experts and systems [12], isolated management and tool-only theory.

Perhaps because the term data governance is too broad, or perhaps the failure cases of enterprises are often digested and internal, although most governance practitioners are deeply aware of the difficulty of data governance work, the author does not find too many case literature on the Internet that analyzes the causes of enterprise data governance failures. In the limited data, most of the failures of data governance will be attributed to the complexity of inter-departmental coordination or the lack of attention from the top management, but what we need to further analyze is the reason behind the "why", why the top management does not realize the importance of data governance? Is it the cost of input that does not agree? Or is there disagreement with the effectiveness of data governance?If the problem lies in the "hull" (technical platform investment) is too large, you should consider analyzing whether the development between "sails" (application scenarios) or "sea" (organizational support) matches, and if enterprises are unable to form a good data culture, they should think about whether the goal of the enterprise to initiate data governance before carrying out cultural guidance is clear, and whether employees can realize the importance of data governance (whether there is a clear "wind" and "tower" to guide the organization to clarify the goal) (Fig. 3).

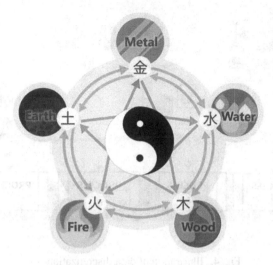

Fig. 3. Yin Yang Five Elements Balance Chart

In ancient Chinese philosophical and medical literature, yin and yang and the five elements are used to explain the relationship between the balance of elements in the universe, and in the Tibetan medical system, diseases are also believed to be caused by the imbalance between the four basic elements and three original sins of the human body. In the same way, data governance is also treating the disease of enterprises, and every practitioner is a doctor, and it is solving the problem of "data" being unable to effectively digest the delicious food of "data" in the enterprise through data governance. In the link of how to analyze and solve problems, practitioners should establish a basic thinking framework, which is also the meaning behind the author's construction of voyage chart. Although each company's data governance fail has its own special reasons, when viewed as a whole, you can try to refer to the concept of mutual promotion and checks and balances in the voyage chart for analysis and interpretation.

4   The Key to Data Governance Capabilities: Wait for the Wind

How to effectively initiate data governance? Some scholars believe that data governance should be laid out in advance, but according to practical visits, it is found that the failure rate of large-scale data governance without clear goals is very high. The driving force in the voyage chart is definitely the first element, if there is no wind and lighthouse, there is no need to build a ship, and building a ship must have a clear motivation and purpose to start.

According to the author's observation and reference to the relevant literature on data management maturity [13, 14], it is found that most of the data management capabilities of enterprises go through three stages, namely data discretization, data centralization, and data systematization (data intelligence may be developed in the future) (Fig. 4).

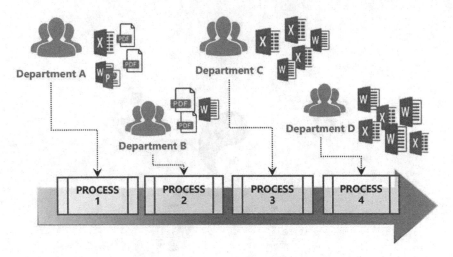

Fig. 4. Illustration of data discretization

The characteristics of data discretization are based on computer office and preliminary informatization, the use and exchange of data is more dependent on office software and mail at this time, even if the system is only used for processes, and the role of information system is closer to "notification" at this stage, the enterprise data in an unstructured form scattered in the computer of each department, managed by each department, data essentially can not form assets (Fig. 5).

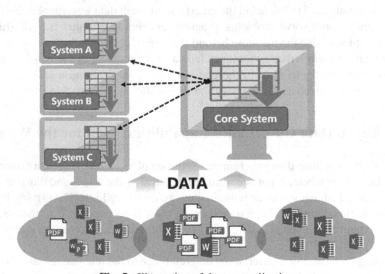

Fig. 5. Illustration of data centralization

Data centralization reflected in the enterprise data gradually from discrete storage to the core of the main system concentration, the proportion of offline data has a relatively obvious reduction, information system to a combination of processes and functions to provide services, at this stage of the demand for data application began to emerge, but this stage of data is still regarded as an accessory of the system, lack of clear data management functions, most enterprises are in this stage, and because the influencing factors of this stage are too complex. A large amount of historical data will be generated at this stage, and most of the prototypes of data management concepts will germinate here. Since the quality of development within this stage largely determines the time of an enterprise transfer to the next management stage (Fig. 6).

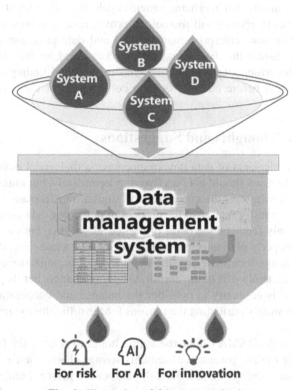

Fig. 6. Illustration of data systematization

The characteristics of data systematization is to manage data management as a special work in a more independent way, data is no longer as an accessory to a system, but by a full-time team or individual to observe, optimize and start to build related data capabilities, this stage is the development direction of most enterprises, at this time should begin to cultivate the data awareness of employees in the enterprise, and the organization should establish a corresponding organization to make decisions on matters involving data.

Although this article starts from the financial leasing industry, enterprises in various industries should clearly position the current stage before starting, look for the direction and goals that meet the characteristics of their own enterprises and recognized by the top management, and the clear goals will help promote the organization to start thinking about how to establish a data strategy and establish a data culture, and there are application scenarios that are gradually decomposed to achieve the goals, and then carry out a series of work such as digital construction to support the scenes. In the absence of driving force, even if the three elements of "ship", "sail" and "sea" are already available, this ship that can never leave port and will continue to waste the cost and energy of the enterprise.

Based on the concept of balanced elements in the framework of long-distance charts, the construction rhythm of targeted deployment and construction can be carried out when carrying out the construction of data management capabilities, and identifying the impact of governance factors in advance will also help improve the success probability of project implementation. For now, enterprise management and data governance practitioners should seriously consider the data management goals faced by the enterprise, avoid the situation of one wrong step and another, and recommend finding and reaching a consensus on the goal before carrying out the construction of the data management system.

5   Conclusion: Thoughts and Suggestions

In a word, the five elements of data governance have a dialectical development relationship, and the elements should not be viewed independently, but interdependent and promoted. Data governance is the cornerstone of digital transformation success and a major challenge for transformation, in the process of practicing data governance, enterprises should not only focus on the latest digital developments, but more importantly, consider how to properly plan to achieve the goals. At the same time, data practitioners also need to change their concepts, the cultivation of organizational structure and digital thinking is certainly part of the corporate culture change, but its process is slow and arduous, and it is necessary to consider the balance and cooperation of multiple factors, rather than simply attributing the reasons for the difficulty to one-sided reasons or individual factors.

As a member of the DAMA China, the author hopes to achieve the following goals through the sharing of data governance elements-voyage charts: Firstly, based on their own experience and learning of DMBOK 2.0, put forward personal understanding, and continue to improve personal cognition of the data management system. Secondly, with the help of drawing the framework diagram, the dependence between various elements is used to stimulate the discussion and thinking of data governance stakeholders with the relationship between common sense, and further improve the development of data governance capabilities of Chinese enterprises. Thirdly, through the analysis of various elements in the chart, the critical path is found, which provides ideas for subsequent enterprises to practice data governance capacity building. Finally, through knowledge sharing, the Data Management Association is rewarded, and only when everyone has a deep understanding of the characteristics and relationships of data governance elements can they practice a realistic data management system in the enterprise and build a good structure and balance between the elements to maintain its development. I hope that practitioners can jointly contribute to digital transformation and wish the motherland better and better!

References

1. DAMA International, DAMA-DMBOK2.0. Basking Ridge, NEW JERSEY: Technics Publications (2016)
2. Tie, L.: The trend and path of digital transformation of traditional industries. People's Forum Acad. Front. **18**, 13–19 (2019)
3. Yanping, S., Haijun, W.: Financial supply-side structural reform and reconstruction of China's financial leasing industry regulatory model. J. Tianjin Univ. (Social Sci. Edn.) **23**(02), 121–128 (2012)
4. Huawei Data Management Department. China Machine Press, Beijing (2020)
5. Xiufeng, L.: Data Governance: Strategies, Methods. Tools an Practice. China Machine Press, Beijing (2021)
6. Chenyu, Z., Wenchun, W., Xuesong, L.: How digital transformation affects enterprise total factor productivity. Financ. Econ. **42**(07), 114–129 (2021)
7. Xuming, M.: A brief analysis of the compliance management of financial leasing companies under the new regulatory environment. Commerical **2.0**(01), 110–112 (2023)
8. Yaohuai, L., Aravena, P.A.: On privacy issues and ethical countermeasures in financial compliance management under the background of big data. Financ. Theory Pract. **42**(01), 2–9 (2021)
9. Zonghui, A.: Research on the development of financial technology and risk prevention. Financ. Developm. Res. **03**, 81–84 (2018)
10. Yangyang, J., Bing, D., Jin, L.: Research on the improvement path of data literacy of employees in aerospace enterprises. Aerosp. Indus. Manag. **03**, 68–72 (2023)
11. Guangsheng, W.: Reflections on data governance and data quality. Tsinghua Financ. Rev. **05**, 32–34 (2021)
12. .Xing, J.: Seven common mistakes in data governance. Comput. Netw. **47**(22), 37–38 (2021)
13. Sumei, G.: DCMM boosts the construction of digital management systems. Softw. Integrated Circ. **08**, 38–39 (2021)
14. Lan, Y.: Comparative study and enlightenment of data management capability maturity model. Library Inform. Work **64**(13), 51–57 (2020)

Exploration and Practice of Digital Transformation for Small and Medium Sized Enterprises

Shengcai Cao[✉] and Yujie Ding

Huaren Health, Hefei, China
dqrcsc@163.com

Abstract. From the perspective of enterprise functions, during the dynamic deduction process of internal and external business development of the enterprise, we try to explore and answer the overall idea of why small and medium-sized enterprises need digital transformation, when they need digital transformation, and how to carry out digital transformation. Based on the exploration of the aforementioned issues, the practical experience accumulated in the digital construction process of relevant industries is given.

Keywords: Digital Transformation · Small and Medium Enterprises · Organizational Digitalization · Management Functions · Data Center · Transformation Practice

1 Introduction

Nearly 400 years ago, the Western thinker Blaise Pascal said, "Mankind is a reed with thoughts." [1] The most essential difference between human and reed is "thoughts." With the deepening of understanding, the difference between human and other animals has also changed from "people can make and use tools" to "can both do things and think about things".

When focusing on the business development process of an enterprise, it is even more necessary to think about it. The leaders and management teams of enterprises need to always think about: "What to do, how to do it? How to do it better? How well it is actually done?" The torrent of the digital age is coming, requiring enterprises to continuously iterate and think deeply about digitalization. It seems that every company recognizes the necessity and value of digitalization. However, in the catering, medical and other industries where the author has worked, relatively few understand or actually promote digital transformation. And even fewer have achieved expected or exceeded expected results of digital transformation.

If you hope to abstract a universal framework model to solve all the problems encountered by different enterprises in digital transformation, it will inevitably lead to mistakes. This article attempts to focus on the small and medium-sized enterprises involved in the author's career. From the perspective of enterprise functions, it conducts a more detailed

M. Luo and L.-J. Zhang (Eds.): CLOUD 2023, LNCS 14204, pp. 26–36, 2024.
https://doi.org/10.1007/978-3-031-51709-9_3

drill-down and systematic deduction of the overall framework, trying to give an overall idea of the digital transformation of small and medium-sized enterprises, and Several practical suggestions for digital transformation practices.

2   The Functions of the Enterprise and Business Development

In fields where informatization and digitalization progress are relatively slow, most small and medium-sized enterprises' understanding of digital transformation is more focused on buying software or developing systems, that is, the digitization of technology. Those enterprises that have slightly carried out the construction of standardized standards, systems and processes will think that digitalization is the informatization of business processes, and it only focuses on improving local efficiency.

Digital transformation is not a project of single-point breakthroughs. It requires a global architectural thinking to elevate digital transformation to the level of corporate strategy. Ignoring the overall architecture and only pursuing single-point breakthroughs will most likely lead to Simpson's paradox. "Win every battle, but lose the whole war".

Digitalization does not reject single-point breakthroughs, but requires a priority order. There must be a global digital architecture first, and then the architecture is continuously filled and enriched. This filling and enriching process may take the efficiency improvement brought about by a single breakthrough as the entry point. Instead of just focusing on local optimization one after another in the absence of a global architecture.

Therefore, in the author's opinion, digital transformation must be the digitization of the entire organization. Since we are digitizing an enterprise as a whole, we must first recognize the core functions of the enterprise, and then think about the digitization of enterprise business around these functions.

2.1   The Functions of the Enterprise [2]

From the perspective of business administration, the business management process mainly involves four major functions: **Planning Function**, **Organizational Function**, **Leadership Function**, and **Control Function** (see Fig. 1).

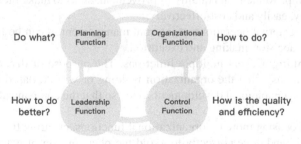

Fig. 1. The four major functions of business management.

1) **Planning Function**: It mainly answers the question of what the enterprise does. It's more about the logic of strategic decision-making, choosing a field, and doing the right thing.
2) **Organizational Function**: It mainly answers the question of what the company should do. After clarifying what to do, it is time to form a team, divide functions, divide labor and cooperate, and think logically to get things done correctly.
3) **Leadership Function**: It mainly answers the question about how the company can do better. There may be thousands of ways to do one thing, but which method is better and more suitable for the enterprise itself requires the enterprise management team to better carry out the evolution of command, coordination, communication, motivation, change and other activities.
4) **Control Function**: It mainly answers the question about how well the company is doing. It is a process of quality management, continuous calibration and correction.

In essence, the overall digital transformation of an enterprise should be based on how these four major functions can better and more efficiently exert value as the starting point for thinking, and continue to carry out cyclic and iterative transformation. Otherwise, it will be difficult for digitalization to become an effective enterprise. There is a big question mark as to whether transformation that is conducive to enterprise development should be carried out. However, in the actual process of enterprise operation and management, these four functions are not separated, but are often connected in series and integrated in every business process. Therefore, in addition to looking at the four major functions involved in the digital transformation of enterprises from a static perspective, we also need to further think about the digital transformation of enterprises from the dynamic process of business development.

2.2 Business Development of the Enterprise

As shown in Fig. 2, the dynamic process of enterprise marketing and management is abstracted and generally includes two major activities: marketing and management.

Marketing: It is an external business development, mainly for incremental growth, pursuit of growth, and efforts to make the existing cake bigger.

Management: It is an internal business development, mainly pursuing cost reduction, efficiency improvement and quality improvement, so as to make more cakes of the same size quickly, easily and cost-effectively.

Whether it is external operations or internal management, it can be further divided into two actions, decision-making and execution.

Decision-making: Covers multiple functions. The purpose of decision-making is to continuously adjust what the organization is doing or will do based on changes in consumer needs, technological developments, etc., so that the company always does the right thing.

Execution: Focusing more on organizational functions, ensuring that decisions can be made correctly and done correctly to avoid the phenomenon of getting everything right in meetings and all wrong in execution.

What kind of decision is the best, or relatively good? What kind of execution is more efficient? How are the implementation effects and control functions implemented, and how are they tested? Whether it is decision-making or execution, there is a pain point that cannot be eradicated, because no one is omniscient and omnipotent. Whether it is decision-making or choosing an implementation method, if we know everything we need to know, we will naturally do our best. But the reality is that there is always an unbridgeable **Information Gap** [3] between what we should know and what we actually know.

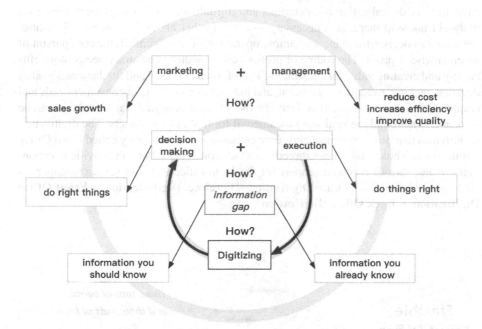

Fig. 2. Business development of the enterprise.

Based on the previous derivation, the most fundamental goal of various optimization methods is to continuously narrow the information gap. Either keep what you should know unchanged and try to increase what you actually know. If you can't increase what you actually know, then find ways to reduce the parts you should know. Of course, in the process of competing with competitors, in addition to narrowing the information gap in absolute terms, as long as we obtain relative comparative advantages, we can also gain more advantages in the competition.

There is definitely more than one solution to narrowing the information gap, but in the digital age, digitization is obviously a relatively better solution. Digitalization, from the continuous accumulation of data during execution, continuously improves the part we actually know; based on the continuously accumulated data, we conduct model construction, business insights, and apply relevant AI algorithms to continuously reduce the parts we should know, so that digitalization back to decision-making. Through such a closed loop, it continues to spiral up, continuously narrows the information gap, and infinitely approaches to bridge the gap between the two, thereby optimizing decision-making and execution, and then optimizing operations and management, helping enterprises to reduce costs, increase efficiency, and improve quality, while obtaining scalable continuous growth.

3　The Overall Idea of Digital Transformation for Small and Medium-Sized Enterprises

Based on the previous dynamic deduction of the internal and external business development of the enterprise, the overall idea of digital transformation [4] can probably have a similar composition, such as digitalization of decision-making and digitalization of execution, or digitalization of operations and digitalization of management. However, it should not stop there. It is necessary to think further about the essence. No matter what kind of decision-making, execution, operation, or management, the core pursuit of an enterprise is profit. The source of profits lies in meeting consumer needs more efficiently and creating value for consumers. Therefore, a common and fundamental goal of decision-making, execution, operation, and management is to meet consumer needs and create value for consumers. Therefore, the overall idea of digital transformation can be broken down around the goal and fundamental foothold of consumers. The digitization of activities that directly contact and serve consumers is customarily called Front Office Digitization. Those that do not directly contact consumers, but can provide decision-making and various resource support for the front office to better serve consumers is customarily called Back Office Digitization. Therefore, **Digitalization = Front Office Digitization + Back Office Digitization**.

Fig. 3. Flexible Front Office.

Front Office Digitalization: Because consumer needs are constantly changing dynamically, and different consumer groups and even individuals have different needs to varying degrees. Therefore, the digitization of the front office must make the front office more flexible and achieve more refined operations around the different arrangements and combinations of the three core elements of people, goods, and place. Different from the traditional one-size-fits-all approach in marketing and store opening, it is replaced by a digital-based "thousands of people, thousands of faces" and "thousands of stores, thousands of strategies" (see Fig. 3).

Back Office Digitization: Different from the front office that directly contacts consumers, the back office is more engaged in carrying out the core value creation activities of the enterprise, as well as some functional support activities around value creation.

The efficient and stable development of these activities has a profound impact on the purchase, sales, and inventory in backend. The combination of existing activity elements, or within the scope of the enterprise ecosystem, puts forward a more robust demand for the digitalization of the supply chain (see Fig. 4).

Fig. 4. Steady Back Office.

Here, a contradiction arises – "How can the pursuit of a stable and unchanging back office effectively meet the needs of a flexible and changeable front office?" A flexible and changeable front office will definitely put forward changing demands on the back office that pursues stability, thus causing constant impact on the stability of the back office. And a stable and unchanging back office will also inevitably create constraints and obstacles to the flexibility and change of the front office.

Let's look back at the composition of Digitalization mentioned above: **Digitalization = Front Office Digitization + Back Office Digitization**. It seems that a more critical link is missing. There should be something similar to a spring or a shock absorber that can be placed between front office and back office. It can meet the flexible and changeable needs of the front office without directly impacting the stability of the back office. It may have various forms and different names, but its fundamental value must be the same, that is, it can simultaneously meet the flexibility needs of the front office and the robustness of the back office, and alleviate the contradiction between the front office and back office. Here we use a more popular concept in the industry - **Middle Office**.

The middle office is not something forcibly created or grafted, nor is it needed in the early stages of enterprise development. It must accompany the continuous development of the enterprise's business. In the process of continuous pulling and running-in between the front office and the back office, with the pursuit of flexibility. The contradiction with the pursuit of stability has become more and more irreconcilable, and it naturally arises. It is a kind of existence that an enterprise should have when it develops to a certain stage.

Middle Office: It must have grown naturally from the digitalization process of the front office and back office. It is a flexible existence that can well integrate the flexible and changeable purchase of people, goods, and place, with the pursuit of stable purchase, sales, and inventory together. The existence of the middle office naturally has digital connotations. Based on the accumulation of front office and back office data, thinking about how to use data to empower business has produced the first gear of the middle office - the **Data Center**, based on the consumer demands of the front office, and the abstraction and componentization of core backend capabilities have given rise to the second gear of the middle office—the **Business Center**. The middle office, under the synergy of these two gears, promotes the continuous operation of business digitization and data business closed loop. As shown in Fig. 5, the reason why there is no relatively popular intelligent middle platform here is because in our opinion, with the continuous closed-loop operation of business digitization and data commercialization, as business and data accumulate and settle, when the innovation demands of the business are consistent with the development of AI technology, the intelligence of an enterprise will naturally emerge. Similar to the concept of a higher-dimensional middle office, the intelligent middle office should not be forcibly attached or grafted.

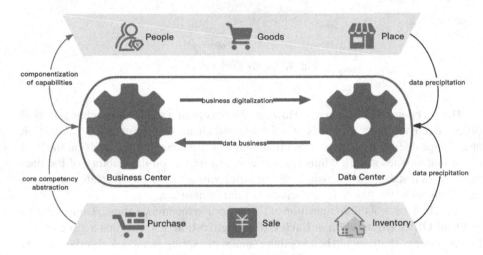

Fig. 5. Digital Middle Office.

At this point, the complete idea of enterprise digitalization has been further expanded to: **Digitalization = Front Office Digitalization + Digital Middle Office + Back Office Digitalization**. The digitalization of the front office is constantly evolving based on the company's own business and consumer needs. The digitalization of the back office is constantly solidified and precipitated based on the company's core value creation activities and supporting functional divisions. As for whether a middle office is needed, or when is a middle station needed? It's determined by the development and changes in the contradiction between the front office and the back office. Moreover, once there is a need for a middle office, it must be based on the core capabilities and business demands of the enterprise. The naturally grown middle office naturally possesses enterprise genes and digital genes.

4 Practical Suggestions for Digital Transformation of Small and Medium-Sized Enterprises

Based on our experience in the transportation field, judicial field, catering field and medical field, as well as some digital transformation practices that we has directly or indirectly participated in, some practical suggestions have been compiled. In our opinion, these practical suggestions cannot guide enterprises in the entire process of digital transformation. They are more extracted from the pitfalls and detours taken. They can be regarded as exhortations to avoid known failures.

4.1 Meet the Needs of Consumer

This suggestion seems to be nonsense. After all, the core of a company's continued existence is to continue to meet the needs of consumers. But in our case, the complete statement of this advice is, "You think you have met the needs of customers, but in fact you have only met the needs that customers think you can meet and that you happen to be able to meet." What I want to express here is actually a more essential thinking about the "Place" in the context of **New Retail** [5]. If you simply use online stores on public platforms or private platforms as a supplement to the sales channels of offline physical stores, it means that you do not understand the essence of **New Retail** at all. Different place must be positioned differently. Asset-heavy physical stores always have their value, but they should be transformed to meet customers' experience needs.

Taking the pharmaceutical distribution industry where we are currently working as an example, the offline physical stores of chain pharmacies must be more focused on providing patients with professional and warm pharmaceutical services. Online stores must understand and meet the potential needs of customers. Based on the fusion analysis of user behavior data and transaction data in online stores, we can gain insight into more customers' needs that they really want to be satisfied, not just the needs that customers have already satisfied. For example, when most patients search for drugs that may be associated with epidemic diseases, it is necessary to promptly reserve the epidemic drugs needed by patients online and offline. When many patients search for drugs that are not available in stores; the probability is that the store needs to replenish the category in time. When the patient has added the drugs to the shopping cart but has not placed an order, the high probability is that the patient needs the medicine but the price is a bit expensive. Due to the seasonality of the disease, the pharmaceutical circulation field also has natural seasonality, we can also early sense the arrival of seasonality from patients' online searching, ordering and other data, and become the first prophet to know about the warmth of spring river water.

Based on offline and warm professional services, we can attract customers to online; based on the exploration of online behavioral data and transaction data, we can perceive more potential customer needs earlier and more comprehensively, thereby creating more marketing contact points for enterprises.

4.2 Don't Do Inefficient Duplication, Do Low-Cost Duplication

Especially for chain-operated small and medium-sized enterprises, in the era of thousands and thousands of stores, if they rely too much on the quality and ability of personnel, the demand for personnel will continue to expand, and the gap of high-quality and high-level talents will definitely become a bottleneck restricting the expansion of enterprises. What we must think about is how to carry out low-cost replication and hand over a large amount of repetitive work to systems and machines, while the value of people is more used in various "non-standard" and "exceptional" transaction processing.

Therefore, enterprises must establish standards, systems, and processes that support rapid replication, and use digital tools to make them online and automated, so as to realize the organizational precipitation of experience and knowledge, and transform personal "knowledge" into organizational "capabilities".

4.3 Don't Buy Software Systems Blindly

Based on the previous deduction of the overall idea of digitalization, it can be naturally concluded that **Digitalization ≠ Buying Software System**, whether it is the digital-ization of the front office, the digitalization of the back office, or the middle office, it must be constantly changing in the development process of the enterprise, and it must keep pace with the development of the enterprise. And it must be closely integrated with businesses of the enterprise.

In addition, in the industries that we had served, there is more or less over-mythology of digitalization. The most intuitive manifestation is that there are problems in business that business people don't understand, and they place their hopes on a certain set of software solutions, naively thought that if some software was bought, the problem would be solved itself. This approach is a typical putting the cart before the horse.

Business is the core, and value creation activities are the guide for all other functional support activities. The system must first better serve the business, and then explore the integration of industry and technology, so as to better lead the business to find innovative development directions, not the system. Stronger or higher than business.

Don't blindly buy software system. It doesn't mean you shouldn't buy software system. It's just that when making decisions about purchasing or developing systems, you should notice that every local optimization you make now creates opportunities for the future, but also imposes certain restrictions. Path dependence caused by sunk costs may even prematurely limit or deprive enterprises of opportunities for better development in the future.

4.4 Construction of Closed-Loop Operations [6]

Before enterprises carry out digital construction, they must pay attention to connecting the planning, organization, leadership, and control functions in series.

For the closed-loop management of internal repetitive matters, the PDCA [7] quality management model can be introduced in a lean way to ensure that the company is doing things right, based on the closed loop of Plan-Do-Check-Act and keeping getting spiraling.

For externally-oriented closed-loop management that responds to the changing needs of the market, the OODA [8] management model can be introduced to avoid enterprises falling into rigidity and losing touch with market changes. It is timely to discover that due to changes in the market and consumer demand, what the company is doing is no longer correct, or due to the revolutionary development of technology, what was done correctly before can become more correct. This enables timely adjustments to organizational decisions, drives the company's organizational innovation, and ensures that the company is always doing the right things.

4.5 Introduction of External Brain

Based on the logic of the curse of knowledge [9], from within the company, it is difficult to see the irrationality that we take for granted because we are used to it.

Once employees and companies develop habits, they will not be able to do things they accept and are forced to do things they are accustomed to, and they will even reject those good intentions that they think are "I am doing it for your own good." optimization changes because those changes require them to change their habits.

Just like the evolutionary logic of life, natural selection means survival of the fittest, not the survival of the strong. The digitalization of an enterprise also starts from the standards, processes and business it has already developed, and selects or builds the system software that is most suitable for the enterprise itself, rather than the most expensive or the best.

The digital transformation that is most suitable for a specific enterprise must not be grafted from elsewhere, or the stacking of various system software, it is digitalization that grows naturally based on the enterprise's own organizational model and business development.

5 Conclusion

Every company can defeat its competitors one after another by continuously strengthening itself. But they will all encounter an existence that is always invincible, and that is the era in which the company is living. Just like a hero of great strength, perhaps he can lift mountains, even hold up Mount Tai and cross the North Sea, but he can never lift himself up. Every enterprise is not only in the current of the times, but also unconsciously becomes a part of the current of the times. Naturally, enterprises cannot surpass or defeat the era in which they live.

Every enterprise will or will eventually encounter resistance, bottlenecks or ceilings in its own development. Digital transformation may not be the only solution to the problems enterprises encounter, but in the digital age we are already in, digital transformation must be a relatively optimal solution.

Digital transformation is an overall strategy involving awareness, organization, business, technology and other aspects. It is a systematic project of genetic reshaping that has slow onset but long-term effect. These characteristics also determine that digitalization is not a strong medicine that can revive the dead in troubled times, but more like a good medicine that can make incremental improvements in governing the world.

For digital transformation, transformation in consciousness, technology, and organization is relatively simple. The difficulty lies in grasping the timing, angle, and method of entry. If you invest too early, you will face huge sunk costs and opportunity costs due to path dependence in the later stage. But if you invest too late, you will face the possibility of dying from a disease without a cure and it will be too late to regret it. When is the best entry point for an enterprise's digital transformation? Enterprises need to take into account their own realities and adapt to local conditions, relying more on the strategic vision and decisive wisdom of enterprise leaders.

References

1. Pascal, B.: Sur La Religion Et Sur Quelques Autres Sujets (1670)
2. Blue, R.: Functions of management. J. Am. Soc. Inform. Sci. **40**(2), 135–136 (2007)
3. Sniedovich, M.: A bird's view of info-gap decision theory. J. Risk Finan. **11**(3), 268–283 (2010). https://doi.org/10.1108/15265941011043648
4. Reis, J., Amorim, M., Melão, N., Matos, P.: Digital transformation: a literature review and guidelines for future research. In: Rocha, Á., Adeli, H., Reis, L.P., Costanzo, S. (eds.) World-CIST 2018. AISC, vol. 745, pp. 411–421. Springer, Cham (2018). https://doi.org/10.1007/978-3-319-77703-0_41
5. Xue, X., Gao, J., Wu, S., Wang, S., Feng, Z.: Value-Based Analysis Framework of Crossover Service: A Case Study of New Retail in China. IEEE Trans. Serv. Comput. **15**(1), 83–96, (2022). doi: https://doi.org/10.1109/TSC.2019.2922180
6. Jiawang, X., Zhu, Y., Jiang, B.: Dynamic pricing model for new , used products in the processing of closed-loop supply chain operation. 2010 Chinese Control and Decision Conference, Xuzhou, pp. 442–447 (2010). https://doi.org/10.1109/CCDC.2010.5499020
7. Wikipedia. https://en.wikipedia.org/wiki/PDCA, last edited on 1 July 2023, at 19:08 (UTC)
8. Wikipedia. https://en.wikipedia.org/wiki/OODA_loop, last edited on 12 September 2023, at 06:22 (UTC)
9. Wikipedia. https://en.wikipedia.org/wiki/Curse_of_knowledge, last edited on 27 September 2023, at 17:38 (UTC)

The Role of Metadata in Data Asset Management in Civil Aviation Information Field

Haifeng Liang, Yang Li, Haixu Miao$^{(\boxtimes)}$, and Shaoyong Pang

TravelSky Technology Limited, Beijing 101300, China
{hfliang,liyang,miaohaixu,sypang}@travelsky.com.cn

Abstract. Under the impetus of new-generation information technologies such as big data, artificial intelligence and the industrial internet, the world is accelerating its transition into the digital economy era. In 2021, China articulated its Digital China Strategy, aiming to digitize and make intelligent, driving economic growth and societal progress in China. "Data" as a crucial production factor plays a paramount role in the development of the digital economy. The capability and level of data asset management will largely determine the extent of data utilization and the release of data value. Against this backdrop, an increasing number of enterprises are incorporating data asset management into their strategic plans. Metadata forms the foundation of data asset management and serves as a crucial cornerstone in other related areas. This article introduces the basic situation about data assets in civil aviation information field and explores how metadata plays a role in data asset management within the civil aviation information sector.

Keywords: Metadata · Data Asset Management · Data Asset Catalog

1 Overview of Data Assets in Civil Aviation Information Field

In 2019, China's civil aviation transported 660 million passengers, making China the world's second-largest aviation transportation country. TravelSky (TravelSky Technology Limited), as a leading provider of information technology solutions in the Chinese aviation and tourism industry, occupies a central position in the value chain of aviation travel distribution within the Chinese civil aviation ecosystem, characterized by multiple stakeholders, a long supply chain, and extensive collaboration. As the second-largest Global Distribution System (GDS) globally, TravelSky, with aviation information technology at its core, has long been a dominant player in the provision of information services in the Chinese civil aviation sector. The Passenger Service System (PSS), built and operated by TravelSky provides flights, passengers, business information, and ticket distribution information to domestic and international airlines, airports, and ticket sales agents. Its services encompass various areas, including aviation information technology services, distribution information technology services, aviation settlement, and clearing services. TravelSky processes a wealth of high-value data in the civil aviation industry, such as passenger reservations, sales, and transportation. Leveraging its extensive core data advantage, TravelSky has consistently strived to offer advanced products and information services to industry participants.

© The Author(s), under exclusive license to Springer Nature Switzerland AG 2024
M. Luo and L.-J. Zhang (Eds.): CLOUD 2023, LNCS 14204, pp. 37–49, 2024.
https://doi.org/10.1007/978-3-031-51709-9_4

1.1 Business Segmentation

During the 1970s and 1980s, China civil aviation started its informatization process. The civil aviation information system included a series of business systems involving industry operation and passenger service, such as airline passenger transport system, airport service system, distribution system, cargo system, maintenance system and decision management system [1], as shown in Table 1.

Table 1. Classification of Civil Aviation Information System Services.

System classification	Information contained in the system
Airline passenger systems	Flight scheduling, operation control, seat management, fare management, revenue management, website sales, settlement system, ticket management, sales management, customer relationship, data support, etc.
Airport service systems	Ground operations, passenger check-in, baggage inquiry, aircraft load balance, gate management, travel security, etc.
Distribution systems	GDS distribution management, agent management, tariff calculation, BSP sales, etc.
Cargo systems	Freight strategy, freight revenue, network planning, collection and settlement, sales and service, etc.
Aircraft maintenance systems	Parts management, maintenance programs, ground equipment, etc.
Decision management systems	Decision support, planning support, financial systems, human resources, etc.

With the rapid development of China's civil aviation industry and the continuous progress of information technology, Travelsky has started the construction of a new generation of civil aviation passenger service system. To ensure the efficient, secure, and stable operation of the civil aviation passenger service system, its development underwent top-level planning and design, following a layered architecture and business domains. The entire civil aviation passenger service system consists of hundreds of functional subsystems, designed with high cohesion and loose coupling between systems, ensuring that there is no unauthorized cross-domain access. Ultimately, the China Civil Aviation Passenger Service System is divided into four layers and five domains (as shown in Fig. 1). The four layers includes backend support services, transaction services, interface services, complementary front-end services and service tools, progressing from the backend to the frontend.

The transaction service layer is the core of the civil aviation Passenger Service System. Based on the business process of civil aviation passenger service, it is divided into five domains: product management domain, product display domain, product sales domain, product delivery domain and security inspection domain.

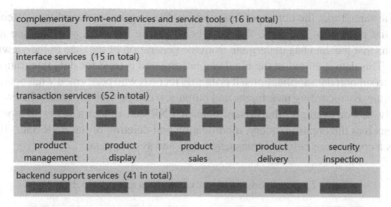

Fig. 1. A demonstration of 4-layer and 5-domain Division Diagram.

Product management domain: including flight inventory control subsystem, flight plan management subsystem, inventory rule management subsystem, seat management subsystem, passenger protection control subsystem, etc.

Product display domain: including flight status query subsystem, fare release subsystem, fare calculation subsystem, etc.

Product sales area: including passenger information service subsystem, reservation management subsystem, electronic ticket sales subsystem, ticket refund and change subsystem, itinerary printing subsystem, electronic invoice subsystem, etc.

Product delivery domain: including departing passengers management subsystem, depart flight control subsystem, load balance control subsystem, etc.

Security inspection domain: including passenger onboard verification subsystem, entry-exit security verification subsystem, etc.

1.2 Data Classification

In the operation of various business systems, two types of data are generated: high-density, high-value business transaction data and system data that reflects the operation of information systems. After years of technical evolution and business accumulation, TravelSky has gradually built an enterprise-level comprehensive big data platform based on a low-cost data warehouse and a commercial big data platform. This platform is used to store both types of data, with a cluster size exceeding 300 servers and a total storage capacity exceeding 7 petabytes (PB).

Transaction data represents the business form of data, which is the state of business as reflected when viewing the data. This data is stored in OLAP databases to support the stable operation of information systems. Taking the reservation system as an example, the entire process of the reservation system involves core business transaction data such as flight inventory data, ticket data, and passenger reservation record(PNR) data. These data are exchanged using predefined messages, with fixed data formats and clear data meanings. For instance, PNR data records passenger reservation details through fixed segments, including name groups, segment groups, contact groups, ticket number groups, contact information groups, special service groups, fare groups, and so on.

At the same time, the corresponding system data is generated, and the system data reflects the process of the data, that is, when viewing the data, you can see all the operations that the data has undergone from the generation of the data to the viewing of the data. This data is stored in the big data platform and is used for data integration and analysis to support data applications. It primarily records who performed what operations at what time. By recording user inputs and outputs, it can be used for user behavior audit and analysis. For example, the system data of PNR can reflect a series of operation records such as the creation, query, modification and deletion of the PNR data. Table 2 provides a comparison between transaction data and system data.

Table 2. Characteristics of transaction data and system data.

Characteristics	Transaction data	System data
Volume of data	Relatively small	Big
Frequency of data generation	Relatively low	High
Data content	High business value	Relatively low business value
Data structure	Structured	Semi-structured, Non-Structure
Data storage	Data Warehouse	Big data platform

With the development approach of "building a large platform, gathering big data, and cultivating a large ecology", under the overall planning of data strategy, the transaction data and system data are managed and processed based on general data technologies and unified data management (see Fig. 2).).

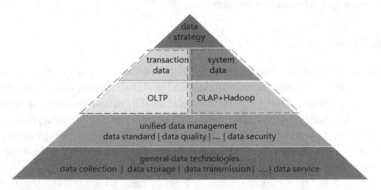

Fig. 2. A framework of transaction data and system data management.

1.3 Metadata in the Domain of Civil Aviation Information

How to conduct data work within such a complex and extensive system, continually explore new civil aviation data application scenarios, facilitate data sharing and utilization, and promote the full realization of data value. The primary question we need to address is: What data exists in the field of civil aviation information? And what is the nature of this data?

Metadata in the field of civil aviation information can answer these questions, providing a description of the data within the civil aviation information domain. At a high level, for instance, in the product management domain, there's flight inventory data and flight schedule data, with their metadata containing details like flight number, operating airline, selling airline, cabin information, etc. In the product sales domain, there are reservation data and ticket data, with metadata that includes reservation time, flight segment information, passenger information, agent information, as well as ticket number, ticket price, and issuance date. In the product delivery domain, data about departing flights and departing passengers include metadata such as departure airport, departure time, number of check-in passengers, baggage weight, and so on (see Fig. 3).

Fig. 3. A demonstration diagram of metadata in the domain of civil aviation information.

Through the collection and centralized storage of the metadata of transaction data and system data, a unified view of the data within the civil aviation passenger service system is formed, which enhances the understanding of data users, and enables them to manage and use data from different perspectives. Metadata management plays a crucial role in the implementation of various areas of data asset management.

2 How Metadata Works

Data asset management encompasses multiple domains, including metadata management, data quality management, data security management, data standards management, and more.These domains work together to maximize the release of data value [2, 3]. Metadata management addresses the challenge of categorizing and managing data within business systems, recording and offering comprehensive data descriptions, and establishing relationships between data, providing robust support and assurance for data asset management.

Metadata can be further categorized into technical metadata, business metadata, operational metadata, management metadata, and security metadata. Technical metadata provides details about the technical aspects of data, the systems that store data, and information about the flow of data within and between systems [4]. Business metadata primarily focuses on the content and conditions of data, including detailed information related to data governance. Business metadata encompasses non-technical names and definitions of subject areas, concepts, entities, attributes, data types, and other characteristics such as scope descriptions, calculation formulas, algorithms, business rules, valid domain values, and their definitions [4]. Operational metadata describes the details of data processing and data access [4]. Management metadata records information related to data ownership and management, including the business and technical management units, personnel, and related work order information. Security metadata provides information about data security attributes, including data security levels and sensitive field information contained in the data. In the following, we will use the familiar example of data warehouse table metadata, as shown in Fig. 4, to illustrate the role of metadata in the following aspects.

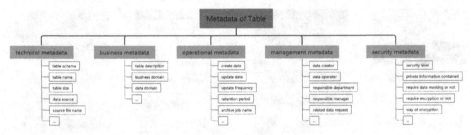

Fig. 4. A demonstration diagram of metadata, illustrated by table's metadata.

2.1 Metadata Management

Typically, we can collect some technical metadata and operational metadata related to database tables from the data warehouse through technical means from the data warehouse itself and its log information. However, business metadata, management metadata, and security metadata are often scattered across different individuals' and various software tools, making it challenging to have a comprehensive understanding of a database table. When you expand this challenge to the thousands of tables in an entire data warehouse, the situation becomes even more daunting.

Currently, there are two main methods of metadata management: proactive (designed) metadata management and reactive (implemented) metadata management. Both methods require the management of a metadata model and the collection of relevant metadata information in accordance with the metadata model. The difference lies in that proactive metadata management is conducted during the data design phase and is primarily achieved through manual completion of forms or metadata model template documents. On the other hand, reactive metadata management is carried out after data is deployed and relies on configuring different types of collection adapters to automate metadata collection. Proactive metadata management requires robust management support and relies on a top-down driving force, strictly following established processes to complete metadata collection. Its downside is its heavy reliance on management intensity and manual maintenance, which leads to high labor costs and insufficient guarantees of the ongoing accuracy, completeness, and integrity of metadata management. Reactive metadata management, on the other hand, collects metadata through technical means after data deployment, ensuring a high level of consistency between the collected metadata and the production environment. However, due to limitations in the production environment, some business metadata, management metadata, and other metadata may not be accessible through technical means. Some technical methods consider adding manual data entry to address this issue, but this approach can reduce work efficiency and make it challenging to ensure metadata management's completeness.

Therefore, we consider forming a closed-loop metadata management system through a combination of proactive metadata registration (designed) and reactive metadata collection (implemented) [5] (see Fig. 5). Both metadata registration and metadata collection adhere to and maintain the same metadata model, allowing for integration and comparison based on this model, thereby achieving centralized metadata management.

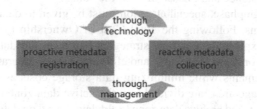

Fig. 5. A closed-loop of metadata management.

Mutual Complementation. Before the data collection team and data service team embark on specific data-related tasks, it is essential to establish a unified metadata registration process. During this process, metadata registration can complement the limitations of technical means in metadata collection, particularly regarding the registration of business metadata, management metadata, and security metadata. This is crucial for enhancing the overall data description. Metadata collection, on the other hand, simplifies the workload of personnel involved in metadata registration and ensures data accuracy. For instance, certain management metadata and operational metadata can be obtained through metadata collection at a later stage without the need for prior registration.

Both complement each other, providing a comprehensive and complete set of metadata for users to query, allowing for a thorough understanding of the data.Both complement each other, providing a comprehensive and complete set of metadata for users to query, allowing for a thorough understanding of the data.

Mutual Validation. Metadata validation can be further categorized into two types: two-state difference analysis and version difference analysis.

Two-state difference analysis compares registered metadata (designed) with collected metadata (implemented) to determine if they match. This helps identify situations where tables were created directly in the backend without proper registration (bypassing the metadata registration process) and alerts and corrective actions are needed for such tables.

Version difference analysis involves comparing the most current version of metadata with the previous version. By examining the differences between these two versions, intelligent monitoring of the data warehouse can be achieved. This allows for timely updates, such as how many tables are added daily, identifying tables that exceed a set threshold (e.g., 1GB), and tracking changes in the space allocation for different data categories. The monitoring results can be periodically communicated to relevant personnel through the design of front-end display pages or email reports.

2.2 Data Lifecycle Management

For data lifecycle management, it needs to be integrated throughout various stages of data work, encompassing data collection, data storage, data processing, and data services. Particularly in the context of data storage and data services, effective data lifecycle management is crucial. Good data lifecycle management ensures data timeliness and helps prevent the existence and misuse of "zombie" data.

In the data storage phase, special attention must be given to data storage costs and data security concerns. Following the Total Cost of Ownership (TCO) concept, it is crucial to actively explore data storage strategies based on the data lifecycle. These strategies should not only ensure reliable and efficient business operations but also meet data security requirements while minimizing data storage costs as much as possible. Ultimately, data storage areas are divided into the active data zone (hot data), inactive data zone (warm data), and archive data zone (cold data) based on data access frequency, importance, and relevant data security requirements. These zones are managed in a rolling manner over time. Different access principles and processes are established for data in different storage zones, and regular audits are organized to monitor data access. Taking Table 3 as an example, for reservation data, departure data, flight inventory data, and ticket data, archive rules determined by the relevant business are applied to facilitate the transition of data from hot to warm and then to cold data.

Table 3. Archive rules for difference kind of data.

Data Classification	Archive rules
Reservation data	Retain for N1 months based on the purge date of the PNR and archive for disposal upon expiration
Departure data	Retained for N2 months based on first leg departure date of flight and archived upon expiration
Flight inventory data	Retained for N3 months based on date of data extraction and archived upon expiration
Ticket data	Retained for N4 months based on date of data extraction and archived upon expiration
Temporary data	Temporary table created by personal account retained for only one month based on the date of creation, automatically deleted upon expiration

In the data service phase, as of now, based on high-value core business transaction data, data services and data value exploration support have been provided to industry clients such as airlines, airports, and agents. This has been achieved through the implementation of 43 categories of data push and query API interfaces, with a daily message volume totaling over 540 million, a TPS of 15,000, over 1,000 daily file counts, and data size close to 400GB. Each type of data provided to external parties (including file services/subscription services) requires a clear business agreement and authorization to ensure that demands are met and responsibilities are clearly defined. The agreements stipulate the necessity of specifying a definite data service period, and they support automated monitoring of the data service end date. Prior to the service's expiration, reminders are sent to relevant personnel, and after the service period has expired, data services are terminated.

Through metadata management, we particularly emphasize the retrieval of metadata information related to "data retention periods" and "data service durations" during the metadata registration process, requiring data lifecycle-related metadata to be mandatory fields. At the inception of data creation, the data collection team or data service team must determine the lifecycle of data, define archiving rules, and provide data handling methods or tools for archiving.

2.3 Data Asset Catalog

The data asset catalog is not a simple listing and display of the full set of system metadata, as not all data qualifies as data assets. Data refers to any electronically or otherwise recorded information. An organization's data encompasses various types of information carriers generated through business and production activities, as well as information carriers specific to the enterprise's business and technical expertise. Data resources refer to organizing raw data to create a scale of data resources that can be processed and developed by the enterprise. Data assets, built upon data resources, through ownership determination, assessment, and other processes, have quantifiable value and can be applied and monetized. Data capitalization assigns financial attributes to data, and data becomes a core force in the capital market. The process from data to data resources transforms unordered and chaotic data into ordered and valuable data, while the process from data resources to data assets realizes the monetization of data value through value exchange and transfer (see Fig. 6).

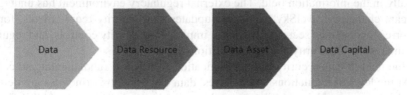

Fig. 6. Evolution of data to data capital.

As shown in Fig. 7, the data asset catalog, built upon a unified metadata management foundation, uses label management to filter and classify metadata. Through the data asset catalog publishing process, we obtain two data directories: the Data Integration and Sharing Directory and the Data Open Sharing Directory. The Data Integration and Sharing Directory answers the question of "what data do we have" in the civil aviation information domain. Using this directory, data can be made interoperable or directly applied. The Data Open Sharing Directory answers the question of "what data can be provided" in the civil aviation information domain. With this open sharing directory, users can directly select the required data and apply for usage rights.

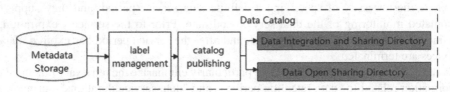

Fig. 7. A demonstration of the relationship between metadata and data asset catalog.

Similarly, the data asset catalog maintains a responsible person for each data asset, and data assets should be managed in the same way as physical assets. Changes in the responsible person (such as resignations or job reassignments) should also involve the transfer and confirmation of their assigned data assets.

2.4 Data Security

The advancement of information technology has made intelligent and smart data applications possible. Travelsky provides data support for a range of emerging businesses, including intelligent passenger travel, precise airline marketing, and smart airports. This has resulted in more extensive and precise data outreach, with profound implications for data security from a business perspective. Furthermore, with the introduction of relevant international and domestic laws and regulations, external data security oversight requirements have become more stringent. A series of laws and regulations, primarily including the "Cybersecurity Law of the People's Republic of China", "Data Security Law of the People's Republic of China", "Personal Information Protection Law of the People's Republic of China" and "Regulations on the Security Protection of Key Information Infrastructure" have been formally issued, imposing higher requirements on security, especially in the information field. The external regulatory environment has undergone significant changes. TravelSky tracks and updates data security requirements, formulates corresponding data security strategies, implements security controls, and regularly audits the results of security strategy execution.

In the field of data security, data classification is the most fundamental and critical task. At the level of regulations and policies, data classification principles are defined, and data is categorized based on data type, data granularity, data scope, and other factors. The extent of harm caused by data leaks, tampering, destruction, illegal access, illegal use, and illegal sharing is determined. TravelSky classifies data security levels into Public Data (Level 1), Restricted Data (Level 2), and Confidential Data (Level 3), and clearly defines the security requirements for each level. Public Data (Level 1) can be accessed by any user of the passenger service system without protective measures. Restricted Data (Level 2) can be accessed by a limited number of users of the passenger service system, and certain protective measures may be required as per civil aviation conventions or airline requirements. Confidential Data (Level 3) can only be accessed by strictly limited users of the passenger service system, and its unauthorized disclosure can lead to legal consequences such as the leakage of passenger personal information data, or it may be required to be protected as per industry standards. It is essential to follow a consistent data classification principle within the enterprise.

At the implementation level, data classification is based on the data asset catalog, which involves a comprehensive investigation and assessment of enterprise data assets. This process clarifies data asset types, data asset distribution, data asset permissions, and data asset usage. During the metadata registration phase, relevant metadata for data classification is recorded and registered. The system determines the minimum granularity of data items contained in each data type. If the included data items match passenger personal information categories (such as name, identification numbers, financial status, travel records, contact information, seat information, travel documents, and biometric data), automatic data risk classification labeling is applied to the data. Throughout the entire data asset management environment, data security labels are bound to data, supporting data retrieval based on different classifications and levels.

In the data storage phase, data security labels are used to determine whether encryption storage technology is necessary, such as encrypting private passenger data while supporting domestic encryption algorithms. In the data processing phase, data application and management are referenced based on data security labels, implementing different data processing strategies. In the data service phase, data authorization management is conducted according to data security labels. Data desensitization may also be applied as needed, such as transforming sensitive information (e.g., passenger sensitive information: identification, payment card numbers, phone numbers, frequent flyer numbers, names, emails) through desensitization rules when moving from a production environment to non-production environments (development, testing, research platforms, etc.). This ensures the confidentiality and availability of sensitive privacy data and provides reliable protection for sensitive privacy data.

3 Conclusion

The capability and proficiency of data asset management will significantly determine the extent of data utilization and the release of data value. Therefore, the importance of data asset management in the civil aviation information field is self-evident [6]. To establish a more systematic, tool-based, and automated management capability, specific objectives are set for each phase of data asset management system development, as depicted in Fig. 8.

Metadata management addresses the issue of "under management" and marks the first step in data asset management, serving as the foundational cornerstone for other management domains. However, achieving effective "well-managed" relies on data standards management. Through metadata management, we can accurately reflect the data landscape in the civil aviation information field, but the quality of metadata, such as the

Fig. 8. Objectives in the development of the data asset management system.

absence of business metadata or inconsistencies in technical metadata, can impact the support capabilities of metadata management for other management areas. Based on the foundation of IATA NDC/ONE Order and considering the characteristics of domestic civil aviation operations, in line with the industry's trend towards openness and retailing, TravelSky has established a unified flight data standard, OFS (One Flight Standard). This standard covers various aspects, including airline flight control, inventory management, flight sales, and flight delivery. It views flights as a complete and unified entity from the perspective of airline business, standardizing and describing business data at all stages of a flight's lifecycle and regulating the data content related to flight business objects. Additionally, a unified passenger data standard, ORS (One Record Standard), has been created. It includes passenger itinerary booking, ticketing, departure check-in, and other business stages, defining the data structure for passenger journey records from both a business and user perspective. Therefore, the next step will be to promote the joint action and cooperation between metadata management and data standardization, to constitute the core functions of the data asset management system.

To achieve the "create value" effect, it is essential to fully consider the current state of the civil aviation information field, coordinate the various functional domains of data asset management, improve data management maturity, provide users with unified, standardized, and easily understandable data asset presentations, enhance data development and application efficiency, and increase the capability for open data sharing.

Additionally, in 2021, Gartner discontinued the traditional metadata management magic quadrant and introduced the concept of Active Metadata for the first time, representing the next generation of data management development. In the future, there will be exploration into a more proactive and dynamic approach, utilizing advanced AI technology for continuous analysis of relationships among various types and vast quantities of metadata. This will provide the capability for automated discovery, analysis, and application of metadata, making metadata management more intelligent and offering better support for data management.

References

1. Peng, M.: Computer Engineering.: Current Situation and Development Outlook of Civil Aviation Information System in China. J. **2005**(07), 61–63 (2005)
2. Mei, H.: Scientific Chinese.: building a data governance system Fostering a data factor market ecosystem. J. **2016**(06), 36–37 (2016)
3. Big Data Standards Working Group of the National Information Standards Committee, F.: Data Management Capability Maturity Assessment Model (2018)
4. Data International T: DAMA Data Management Body of Knowledge. 2nd. Technics Publications, Westfield (2017)

5. Standardization Administration, Information technology Metadata registration system (2009)
6. Lu, J.: Civil-Military Integration on cyberspace.: new dynamics of data governance new development of intelligent civil aviation. J. **2021**(07), 10–11 (2021)

Blockchain-Driven Dog Care System: Leveraging NFTs, IPFS, and Smart Contracts for Advanced Dog Medical Record Management

Duy D. X. Pham[1(✉)], Khoa T. Dang[1], Hieu M. Doan[1], Nam B. Tran[1], Bang L. Khanh[1], Nguyen D. P. Trong[1], and Ngan N. T. Kim[2]

[1] FPT University, Can Tho, Vietnam
duypdxse161418@fpt.edu.vn
[2] FPT Polytecnic, Can Tho, Vietnam

Abstract. The domain of dog healthcare is undergoing transformative change, demanding more robust systems for ensuring the accuracy, retrievability, and protection of medical records. This paper unveils an innovative paradigm for advancing traditional dog medical data management using blockchain technology. Capitalizing on Non-Fungible Tokens (NFTs), the InterPlanetary File System (IPFS), and Smart Contracts, we propose a system that refines data retrieval and modification processes, bolstering both visibility and trustworthiness. At the heart of our solution is a pioneering decentralized structure, empowering veterinarians to register, retrieve, and alter medical records, with every action governed by rigorous access barriers and identity confirmation methods. The distributed characteristics of IPFS offer resilient, alteration-resistant data retention, whereas the NFTs encapsulate the individuality of each dog's medical journey. The incorporation of Smart Contracts ensures fluid data modifications, preserving a distinct and unchangeable chronicle of medical histories. Set against traditional frameworks, our model ensures superior security, adept data stewardship, and unmatched clarity, signposting the future of dog healthcare.

Keywords: Dog Care System · Dog Medical Record · Blockchain · Smart Contracts · NFT · IPFS · BNB Smart Chain · Celo · Fantom · Polygon

1 Introduction

The digital transformation has deeply influenced many sectors, including healthcare. For humans, the significance of electronic health records (EHRs) has become apparent [5,6]. These digital solutions streamline patient care, facilitate improved decision-making, and drive forward research endeavors. In a parallel realm, veterinary practices have also embraced the digital wave, especially concerning dog healthcare and wellness. The implications and advantages of electronic health records tailored for dogs, our faithful companions, have become subjects of intensive exploration [23]. These digital archives not only serve as repositories but have evolved into pivotal instruments in advancing canine health and research.

Demographics of pets and their medical histories play a pivotal role in determining health trends, identifying common ailments, and making informed decisions regarding treatment. The work of [11,20] sheds light on demographics and the major medical causes affecting pets, highlighting the importance of having reliable and comprehensive Electronic Dog Medical Records (EDMRs). As obesity emerges as a significant concern in pet health [7], accurate records can be instrumental in addressing and monitoring this issue.

Furthermore, the quality and accuracy of medical records directly influence health-related welfare prioritization [24]. It's not just about tracking typical health parameters. The nuanced areas, like understanding the intricacies around euthanasia decision-making as documented by [8], emphasize the depth and breadth of information that EDMRs can potentially encapsulate.

The utilization of EDMRs isn't limited to health diagnoses or treatment plans. Syndromic surveillance, as explored by [3,10], showcases the potential of EDMRs in epidemiological tracking and disease outbreak predictions. Ticks and animal bites, often sidelined, have been highlighted as areas of significant concern [9,17,26].

However, these advancements in dog health digitalization do not come without challenges. Data management, quality, and access control are hurdles to be reckoned with [16,19]. Inherent flaws exist in the centralized frameworks of traditional EHR systems, making them susceptible to breaches and unauthorized access, all of which compromise the integrity and security of the sensitive data they house [23,25].

Against this backdrop, blockchain emerges as a beacon. Its decentralized, immutable, and transparent nature offers compelling solutions to the constraints of traditional systems. Integrating this with off-chain storage, tokenization, and other auxiliary blockchain tools could revolutionize the way we manage and perceive Dog Medical Records.

Diving deeper, Non-Fungible Tokens (NFTs) bring to the table properties that can encapsulate the unique medical history of each dog. This ensures a transparent, tamper-proof digital representation of every canine's health journey. Complementing this, the InterPlanetary File System (IPFS) promises resilient and decentralized data storage, ensuring persistent and accessible dog medical data. Therefore, this paper aims to contribute:

1. **Blockchain-centric Dog Care System:** A revolutionary framework powered by blockchain for advanced dog healthcare, addressing concerns of data security, integrity, and accessibility.
2. **EDMRs via NFTs:** Utilizing NFTs, we emphasize the transparency and authenticity of each dog's medical record, paving the way for enhanced trust and verification.
3. **IPFS-Powered Dog Medical Data Exchange:** With IPFS, we usher in an era of decentralized data sharing, amplifying collaboration and comprehensive dog care initiatives.

4. **Cross-Platform Proof-of-Concept:** Beyond theoretical propositions, we validate our system by implementing it across BNB Smart Chain, Celo, Fantom, and Polygon, emphasizing its adaptability across varied blockchain environments.
5. **Pinata Platform for Persistent Data Availability:** Leveraging the IPFS-based Pinata platform, we ensure that dog medical records are both persistent and decentralized, ensuring continuity in care and mitigating data loss risks.

2   Related Work

2.1   General Healthcare System for Animal

The intersection of digital technology and animal healthcare has garnered substantial attention in recent years. Notably, the healthcare of dogs, as a specific subset of this domain, has been rigorously explored, yielding crucial insights. These developments can be conceptualized across several thematic clusters, as delineated below:

Demographics, Health Concerns, and Syndromic Surveillance: Emerging from the vast pool of research in this area, [20] furnishes comprehensive data on pet demographics through electronic health records, exclusively focusing on Great Britain. Concurrently, [11] offers a granular perspective on the predominant medical concerns prompting clinic visits for dogs in Korea. Elevating the discourse to a macroscopic level, syndromic surveillance emerges as a significant theme, chiefly for its role in outbreak detection. The foundational principles and methodologies of this surveillance approach are articulated by [10]. Further nuancing this discourse, [3] underscores the integral role played by electronic medical records in facilitating syndromic surveillance endeavors.

Specific Health Challenges and Welfare Prioritization: Transitioning from broad demographic trends to specific health challenges, canine obesity emerges as a pressing concern. The proliferation of this issue is meticulously studied by [7], with a regional focus on New Zealand. Augmenting the health discourse, [24] harnesses electronic health records to prioritize a spectrum of canine disorders within the UK. Moreover, a comprehensive understanding of the pharmaceutical interventions for canine acute diarrhea is provided by [21].

Ethical Decisions and Mental Health Implications: The ethical contours of animal healthcare are profound. Venturing into this delicate territory, [8] navigates the decision-making landscape around euthanasia for both dogs and cats, using electronic health records as a guiding lens. Furthermore, extrapolating the discourse to the implications of animal-human interactions, a salient theme emerges around animal-inflicted injuries. [9] and [17] delve into the phenomenon of animal bites and their intertwined relationship with human mental health.

Data Quality, Access Control, and System Adoption: As digital solutions penetrate veterinary care, concerns around data quality and access control gain prominence. [16] delivers a comprehensive evaluation of the data quality in animal health records, with an emphasis on Swiss dairy farms. Mirroring the concerns in human healthcare, the need for robust access control mechanisms in animal health records is championed by [19]. Providing a ground-level perspective, [1,12] shed light on the adoption rate and practical feasibility of digital systems in veterinary practices.

Text Mining, Spatial Analysis, and Advanced Analytics: Finally, the capability of harnessing advanced analytics in animal healthcare has shown considerable promise. Specifically, [2] accentuates the potency of text mining techniques applied to free-text medical records for enhanced surveillance. Further diversifying analytical approaches, [4] exploits spatial-temporal data to discern patterns in companion animal enteric syndrome.

In conclusion, the burgeoning nexus between digital tools and dog healthcare furnishes a multifaceted landscape. As our research gravitates towards blockchain-centric solutions, it remains indispensable to acknowledge and build on these seminal contributions.

2.2   Blockchain-Based Healthcare System

Blockchain's potential to revolutionize the healthcare domain, particularly in patient-centered systems, has been the focus of various recent studies. A recurrent theme in these studies is the use of blockchain technology to ensure the security and accessibility of patient data, especially during emergencies. Son et al. [22] and Le et al. [13] both emphasize the challenges in traditional access systems during medical emergencies. These studies propose blockchain-based solutions that utilize the permissioned Blockchain Hyperledger Fabric, emphasizing the use of smart contracts to define access rules, ensuring both security and timely access to critical patient data during emergencies.

Furthermore, in the realm of medical data sharing and inter-institutional collaboration, Duong et al. [6] underscore the importance of ensuring only authorized parties access health records. They highlight the limitations of current healthcare systems in guaranteeing this and introduce a patient-centered healthcare system using smart contracts via blockchain technology. This approach is further elaborated by Duong et al. [5], who delve into the technical aspects, detailing algorithms that facilitate data interactions within their proposed system.

Beyond direct patient care, blockchain's application in the broader healthcare supply chain is gaining traction. The management of medical waste, especially in the context of the COVID-19 pandemic, is addressed by Le et al. [15], who propose a decentralized blockchain-based system, the Medical-Waste Chain. This system aims to automate waste treatment processes and foster collaboration between relevant stakeholders. In the sphere of blood donation, both Le et al.

[14] and Quynh et al. [18] recognize the inadequacies of traditional blood management systems. They propose blockchain solutions to offer a more detailed and effective management of blood information, ensuring quality and addressing supply-demand challenges.

3   Approach

3.1   Traditional Dog Care System

The traditional dog care system, while having served its purpose for many years, had several limitations that became evident with the advent of technology. This system primarily relied on face-to-face interactions, paper-based record-keeping, and manual communication channels, offering a more localized approach to care (refer to Fig. 1 for a visual representation).

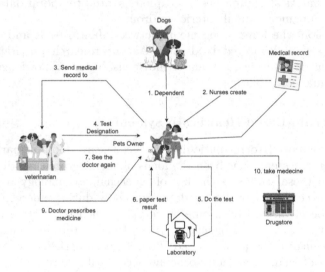

Fig. 1. Traditional system for dog care

Veterinarian - Physical Veterinarian Clinic: The traditional veterinarian clinic was the epicenter of all health-related interactions. Appointments, consultations, and records were managed manually, often requiring physical presence for any form of update or inquiry.

Medical Record - Paper-Based Medical Records (PBMRs): Physical documents and files were the norm. These records, although tangible, posed challenges related to storage, retrieval, loss, or damage.

Dogs: The focus was primarily on general care rather than breed-specific requirements. While regular check-ups were advised, there wasn't a tailored approach that catered to the unique needs of individual dog breeds.

Owners - Dog Owners as Caretakers: In the traditional system, dog owners played a passive role, relying on periodic vet visits for updates and recommendations. They maintained physical vaccination cards and manually tracked medication schedules.

Drugstore - Local Pharmacies: Medications were sourced from local pharmacies based on handwritten prescriptions. This process often involved waiting times and manual verification of drug availability.

Laboratory - Diagnostic Centers: Diagnostic centers operated in isolation. Veterinarians had to manually refer patients, and results were communicated via physical reports, leading to potential delays in treatment.

The traditional dog care system followed these basic steps:

First step: Physical Registration of the Dog - Upon acquiring a dog, owners would register their pet at a local clinic, filling out paper forms detailing their dog's information. **Second step:** In-Clinic Health Examinations - Health examinations were conducted exclusively in-person. Findings were recorded manually and stored in physical files. **Third step:** Prescription of Diagnostic Tests - If tests were needed, vets would provide handwritten referrals. Owners then scheduled appointments in-person or over the phone. **Fourth step:** Collection of Test Results - Owners often returned to diagnostic centers to collect physical test reports, which were then presented to the vet during a follow-up visit. **Fifth step:** Prescription and Medication Collection - Post-diagnosis, vets provided handwritten prescriptions. Owners then procured medications from local pharmacies.

Challenges inherent to the traditional pet care model:

- **Storage and Management of Physical Documents**: The reliance on PBMRs posed issues related to space, potential loss, or damage.
- **Limited Communication**: The absence of direct communication channels could lead to delays in care and miscommunication.
- **Lack of Accessibility**: Physical records meant information couldn't be accessed or shared remotely, complicating specialist consultations.
- **Data Vulnerability**: Paper records were susceptible to damage from natural elements, and there was no backup.
- **Delayed Responses**: A lack of instant notifications often resulted in slower health interventions.
- **Potential for Human Errors**: Handwritten prescriptions and manual record-keeping increased the risk of mistakes.

While the traditional system had its merits and provided foundational practices, it became clear over time that modernizing certain elements would vastly improve efficiency and care quality for our cherished canine companions.

3.2   Blockchain-Enhanced Dog Care System

To surmount the challenges of the traditional dog care model, our approach incorporates a blockchain-based method. Drawing upon cutting-edge technologies such as smart contracts, NFTs (Non-Fungible Tokens), IPFS (InterPlanetary File System), and an intricate blockchain structure, this model offers a significant leap in dog care systems. Figure 2 demonstrates our avant-garde strategy, introducing multiple novel components poised to redefine dog care, ensuring transparency, security, and efficiency.

User Interface. The user interface remains pivotal, acting as the linchpin between veterinarians and the digital database of canine medical records. This digital platform should intuitively facilitate veterinarians in registering medical findings, diagnosing conditions, suggesting treatments, and scheduling revisits. Enriched with tools like graphical visualizations, predictive AI capabilities, and breed-specific care suggestions, the user interface can remarkably uplift the standard of canine healthcare.

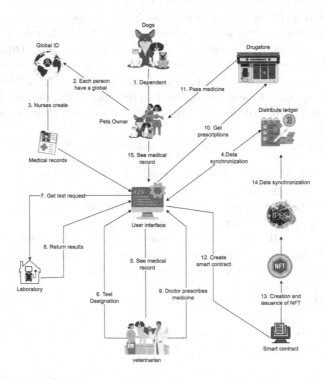

Fig. 2. Blockchain-enhanced model for dog care

Dog Identification Code. Prioritizing data security and privacy, each dog is linked to a distinct Dog Identification Code (DIC). This unique alphanumeric code functions as a digital key, ensuring that only designated individuals like the dog owner or vet can access and update the records, safeguarding data confidentiality.

Smart Contract. In the realm of dog care, the smart contract emerges as an auto-executing digital pact that fortifies the protection, retrieval, and modification of Electronic Dog Medical Records (EDMRs). By laying down predefined protocols and access permissions, it guarantees restricted access, maintaining data sanctity.

NFT (Non-Fungible Token). Visualizing each dog's health record as an NFT metamorphoses the EDMR into a distinct, unalterable digital asset anchored on a blockchain. Beyond assuring authenticity, it eases the transition of data, especially if a dog gets rehomed or sold, ensuring that the health history perpetually accompanies the dog.

IPFS (InterPlanetary File System). The adoption of IPFS for dog medical records endorses the paradigm shift from centralized to decentralized data storage. The redundancy introduced by IPFS amplifies data accessibility, ensuring records remain available even during server downtimes. The cryptographic hashing integrated into IPFS guarantees the immutability of data, countering unauthorized amendments.

Distributed Ledger. Within canine care, the distributed ledger is visualized as a decentralized archive chronicling every health-related transaction concerning a dog. Contrasting with centralized databases, this ledger thrives on consensus algorithms, which authenticate data authenticity and consistency. From vaccination details to surgical notes, every action receives its unique timestamped entry, promoting transparency and traceability.

The process flow, as elaborated in Fig. 2, fuses these components into a coherent 14-step system. This procedure emphasizes enhanced data security, transparency, and efficiency, revitalizing the conventional dog care framework.

This blockchain-centric methodology signifies a transformative step in dog care. Beyond the fundamental advantages of fortified data security, this model delivers unparalleled transparency, solidifies the inviolability of EDMRs, and remarkably streamlines canine care and management. Our proposal, by virtue of its distinct characteristics, rectifies traditional model flaws:

By converging the avant-garde of technology with traditional canine care practices, our blockchain-enhanced approach presents a comprehensive solution for the challenges faced by dog owners, veterinarians, and the larger dog care industry.

4   Assessment

Blockchain's landscape is vast and dynamic, with many platforms now operating under the Ethereum Virtual Machine (EVM) umbrella. Our assessment protocol involves the execution of our intended smart contracts on four EVM-aligned platforms: *Binance Smart Chain*[1], *Polygon*[2], *Fantom*[3], and *Celo*[4]. We're keen to delve into the unique functionalities and prospects of each. Moreover, recognizing the surge in decentralized storage mechanisms and the expanding realm of NFTs, we intend to lodge the essential dog data, specifically their health logs, on IPFS utilizing the *Pinata platform*[5].

4.1   Simulated Ecosystem

In the vast expanse of decentralized systems, nodes play an instrumental role, underpinning data veracity, availability, and protection. Our simulation blueprint is tailored to resonate with the operational cadence of a genuine decentralized blockchain. Figure 3 demonstrates a cohort of 20 nodes, each with distinct cryptographic key pairs, employed for our assessment.

Fig. 3. 20 node cluster (highlighting the starting 5 nodes) with cryptographic keys

Each node in this structure could potentially mirror an entity in the Dog Health Ledger - be it dog enthusiasts, veterinary professionals, or academic bodies. Harnessing an amalgamation of both cloud-based and tangible servers, we've architected a multifaceted testing realm to rigorously assess our system's adaptability and robustness.

---

[1] https://github.com/bnb-chain/whitepaper/blob/master/WHITEPAPER.md.
[2] https://polygon.technology/lightpaper-polygon.pdf.
[3] https://whitepaper.io/document/438/fantom-whitepaper.
[4] https://celo.org/papers/whitepaper.
[5] More on Pinata's developer-friendly IPFS interface: https://www.pinata.cloud/.

4.2   IPFS Integration for Dog Health Logs

IPFS is revolutionizing the ethos of decentralized data warehousing. Our initiative gravitates towards employing IPFS for cataloging Dog Health Logs. This method presents an unyielding and enduring vessel to chronicle indispensable health metrics of dogs. Marrying Pinata's platform with IPFS, we seek to amalgamate streamlined user interaction with steadfast infrastructure.

The display in Fig. 4 elucidates a dog's health log, detailing pivotal metrics including identification, past ailments, immunizations, and pertinent health narratives. A decentralized archival ensures data resilience, fortifying against potential data attrition.

Lastly, Fig. 7 demystifies the extraction methodology. The health log can be summoned from the IPFS mesh using its singular ID or cryptographic hash, underscoring the efficacy and resilience of this mechanism.

Through the fusion of IPFS with dog health logs, we champion a distributed, resilient, and indelible mechanism, facilitating seamless access and dissemination of pivotal dog health narratives among veterinarians, dog aficionados, and pertinent stakeholders.

```
describe("Dog Care System", function () {
    it("Should set the right unlockTime", async function () {
        const { owner, otherAccount, medicalRecord, pinata } = await loadFixture(
            deployOneYearLockFixture
        );

        const body = {
            doctorID: "doctorID 1",
            nurseID: "nurseID 1",
            petID: "petID 1",
            name: "Pet kind (e.g., Cat)",
            Owner: "Owner name",
            Dianose: "Diagnose",
            treatmentHistory: "The past ailments of the dog",
            immunizations: 1,
            dogHealth: "pertinent health narratives",
        };
        const options = {
            pinataMetadata: {
                name: "Electronic Dog Medical Records.json",
            },
            pinataOptions: {
                cidVersion: 0,
            },
        };
```

Fig. 4. Snapshot of a dog's health journal

```
You are using a version of Node.js that is not supported by Hardhat, and it may work incorrectly, or not work at all.

Please, make sure you are using a supported version of Node.js.

To learn more about which versions of Node.js are supported go to https://hardhat.org/nodejs-versions

    lock
        Dog Care System
CID QmbAGX15IpV3sxo4NcjbQfm9XgIg78mxeHXb1xz18fUfP0
            ✓ Should set the right unlockTime (632ms)

    1 passing (6s)
```

Fig. 5. Process of generating a cryptographic hash for a dog's health entry on IPFS

Upon onboarding a dog's health log into the IPFS grid, a cryptographic hash link, as visualized in Fig. 5, is instantiated. This hash facilitates a distributed retrieval mechanism, ensuring data can be effortlessly accessed across the IPFS consortium.

4.3　Testing on EVM-Supported Platforms

Blockchain, as a revolutionary technology, thrives on adaptability, and the Ethereum Virtual Machine (EVM) stands testament to this virtue. Its diverse ecosystem has nurtured an array of platforms, each of which brings distinct capabilities to the table. As we journey forward in our assessment, it becomes pivotal to gauge the efficiency and robustness of our Dog Health Ledger on these EVM-compatible platforms.

Our testing protocol encompasses three key operational facets:

1. **EDMR (Electronic Dog Medical Record) Creation:** This process involves the digitized documentation of a dog's health metrics. It's imperative that this record, being both critical and comprehensive, is created seamlessly across various platforms, ensuring both speed and accuracy.
2. **Mint NFT (Non-Fungible Token):** Beyond just data entry, the uniqueness of each dog's health record warrants representation as an NFT. Minting, or creating, this NFT ensures that the digital representation is both authentic and non-replicable. It's paramount that our system can efficiently produce these tokens without hiccups on all EVM platforms.
3. **Transfer NFT:** The dynamic nature of data, especially in collaborative spaces like pet care, necessitates the seamless transfer of these NFTs among stakeholders. This action could signify a change in ownership, sharing for consultation, or myriad other scenarios. EVM platforms should ensure that such transfers are smooth, rapid, and secure.

Figure 6 portrays the dog's health log's ID conservation process on Pinata, further bolstering its reachability and redundancy.

We shall further dissect and delve into the intricacies of each of these operations in the different scenarios (i.e., the next subsequent sections). It's our objective to not only implement but to optimize these functionalities across the diverse canvas of EVM-supported platforms, thereby ensuring a Dog Health Ledger that's both versatile and efficient.

Fig. 6. Storing the dog's health entry ID on Pinata's ecosystem

```
      maroon-wandering-fly-487.mypi  ×  +
   C      https://maroon-wandering-fly-487.mypinata.cloud/ipfs/QmbbSKt5TpV3zvXMkjbQMYMVgTg7BxuuH/
 1  {
 2      "doctorID": "doctorID 1",
 3      "nurseID": "nurseID 1",
 4      "dogID": "dogID 1",
 5      "name": "Rocky",
 6      "Owner": "John H. F.",
 7      "Dianose": "Diagnose",
 8      "treatmentHistory": "The past ailments of the dog",
 9      "immunizations": 1,
10      "dogHealth": "pertinent health narratives"
11  }
```

Fig. 7. Extraction process of a dog's health journal using its distinct ID

Table 1. Transaction fee

	Pet Medical Record/ Transaction Creation	Mint NFT	Transfer NFT
BNB Smart Chain	0.0273134 BNB ($5.87)	0.00109162 BNB ($0.23)	0.00057003 BNB ($0.12)
Fantom	0.00957754 FTM ($0.001919)	0.000405167 FTM ($0.000081)	0.0002380105 FTM ($0.000048)
Polygon	0.006840710032835408 MATIC($0.00)	0.000289405001852192 MATIC($0.00)	0.000170007501088048 MATIC($0.00)
Celo	0.007097844 CELO ($0.003)	0.0002840812 CELO ($0.000)	0.0001554878 CELO ($0.000)

Transaction Fee Analysis. Table 1 offers a comprehensive view of the transaction fees associated with various operations on the four considered EVM-compatible platforms. Such fees are fundamental to understanding the financial viability of deploying and operating a decentralized application on these platforms.

1. **Dog Medical Record (DMR) Creation:**
   - **BNB Smart Chain:** Charging a fee of 0.0273134 BNB, which is approximately $5.87, the BNB Smart Chain platform stands as a mid-ranged option in terms of cost.
   - **Fantom:** With a fee of 0.00957754 FTM (equivalent to roughly $0.001919), Fantom emerges as a highly cost-effective choice for creating a Dog Medical Record.
   - **Polygon:** The fee levied by Polygon is 0.006840710032835408 MATIC, which due to its low monetary value, doesn't incur any significant cost (practically negligible at $0.00).
   - **Celo:** Charging 0.007097844 CELO, amounting to $0.003, Celo also proves to be a pocket-friendly platform for this operation.
   vbnet Copy code
2. **Minting NFTs:**
   - **BNB Smart Chain:** At a fee of 0.00109162 BNB or approximately $0.23, the BNB Smart Chain remains affordable for minting unique NFTs.
   - **Fantom:** Fantom's fee stands at 0.000405167 FTM, translating to a minuscule $0.000081.
   - **Polygon:** Charging 0.000289405001852192 MATIC with an almost negligible dollar value ($0.00), Polygon emerges as a cost-effective choice.

- **Celo:** With a fee of 0.0002840812 CELO, amounting to practically $0.000, Celo is also an economical option for NFT minting.
3. **NFT Transfers:**
    - **BNB Smart Chain:** The transaction fee on the BNB Smart Chain is 0.00057003 BNB or about $0.12.
    - **Fantom:** For transferring an NFT, Fantom charges 0.0002380105 FTM, which is approximately $0.000048.
    - **Polygon:** Polygon's fee is 0.000170007501088048 MATIC, and its dollar equivalent remains negligible.
    - **Celo:** With a charge of 0.0001554878 CELO, which is roughly $0.000, Celo ensures affordable NFT transfers.

From the presented fees, it's evident that while all platforms maintain competitive pricing structures, certain platforms offer more economical rates for specific operations. Stakeholders need to balance between the transaction fees and the platform-specific features when choosing the optimal platform for their requirements. This comparative analysis aids in making an informed decision by providing a clear picture of the transactional expenses across the EVM-compatible platforms.

Burn Fee. The concept of burning in the cryptocurrency world refers to the act of permanently removing tokens from circulation, effectively reducing the total supply. This is typically achieved by sending the tokens to an unspendable address. Depending on the blockchain platform, burning can sometimes be associated with certain operations, like transaction creation, minting NFTs, or transferring NFTs.

Table 2. Burn fee

	Pet Medical Record/ Transaction Creation	Mint NFT	Transfer NFT
BNB Smart Chain	0.0050316262999993 BNB ($1.08)	0.0011175342 BNB ($0.24)	0.000849245 BNB ($0.18)
Fantom	not mention	not mention	not mention
Polygon	0.000000000032835408 MATIC	0.000000000001852192 MATIC	0.000000000001088048 MATIC
Celo	not mention	not mention	not mention

Table 2 showcases the burn fees across different EVM-compatible platforms for the operations specified in the Dog Health Ledger.

1. **Dog Medical Record (DMR) Creation:**
    - **BNB Smart Chain:** This platform deducts a burn fee of 0.0050316262999993 BNB, equivalent to approximately $1.08.
    - **Fantom:** Fantom does not specify any burn fee for this particular operation.
    - **Polygon:** For each DMR creation, a minimal fee of 0.000000000032835408 MATIC is burnt. Given its low value, this fee is practically negligible in monetary terms.
    - **Celo:** Celo also does not mention a burn fee for DMR creation.

2. **Minting NFTs:**
   - **BNB Smart Chain:** An amount of 0.0011175342 BNB is burnt, translating to about $0.24.
   - **Fantom:** Again, Fantom does not list any burn fee for NFT minting.
   - **Polygon:** Minting an NFT on Polygon will result in a burn fee of 0.000000000001852192 MATIC, which is infinitesimally small.
   - **Celo:** No burn fee is mentioned by Celo for this operation.
3. **NFT Transfers:**
   - **BNB Smart Chain:** A burn fee of 0.000849245 BNB, equivalent to roughly $0.18, is associated with NFT transfers on this platform.
   - **Fantom:** Fantom doesn't specify any burn fee for NFT transfers.
   - **Polygon:** Transferring an NFT on Polygon will burn a minute fee of 0.000000000001088048 MATIC.
   - **Celo:** Celo remains consistent in not specifying a burn fee for this operation as well.

In summarizing the burn fees, the BNB Smart Chain and Polygon platforms have specified amounts that are deducted for the respective operations. In contrast, Fantom and Celo haven't provided any details regarding burn fees. This information becomes essential for users and developers, as burn fees directly influence the overall token circulation and can impact the token's value in the long run. As with transaction fees, understanding burn fees is crucial for making informed decisions about which platform is most suitable for a particular application or use-case.

5 Conclusion

The development and adoption of Electronic Dog Medical Records (EDMRs) bear paramount importance, holding the potential to revolutionize canine health and research. Traditional centralized systems, in all their might, have showcased vulnerabilities, emphasizing the need for more resilient and decentralized solutions. In light of these findings, our paper's contributions pivot on creating a symbiotic relationship between advanced technologies and dog healthcare. By harnessing the power of blockchain, emphasizing the uniqueness of each dog's medical journey through NFTs, and ensuring decentralized and persistent storage through IPFS, we envision a future where canine healthcare is more transparent, secure, and collaborative. With our blockchain-driven dog care system, we hope to set a precedent for advanced, reliable, and decentralized healthcare solutions, not just for our canine companions but as a beacon for broader digital healthcare transformations.

References

1. Aigner, C.: Prototypical implementation of an animal health record (AHR) for livestock management, Ph. D. thesis (2014)

2. Anholt, R.M., et al.: Mining free-text medical records for companion animal enteric syndrome surveillance. Prev. Vet. Med. **113**(4), 417–422 (2014)
3. Anholt, R.: Informatics and the electronic medical record for syndromic surveillance in companion animals: development, application and utility, Ph. D. thesis, University of Calgary (2013)
4. Anholt, R., et al.: Spatial-temporal clustering of companion animal enteric syndrome: detection and investigation through the use of electronic medical records from participating private practices. Epidemiol. Infect. **143**(12), 2547–2558 (2015)
5. Duong-Trung, N., et al.: On components of a patient-centered healthcare system using smart contract. In: Proceedings of the 2020 4th International Conference on Cryptography, Security and Privacy, pp. 31–35 (2020)
6. Duong-Trung, N., et al.: Smart care: integrating blockchain technology into the design of patient-centered healthcare systems. In: Proceedings of the 2020 4th International Conference on Cryptography, Security and Privacy, pp. 105–109 (2020)
7. Gates, M., et al.: Assessing obesity in adult dogs and cats presenting for routine vaccination appointments in the north island of new zealand using electronic medical records data. N. Z. Vet. J. **67**(3), 126–133 (2019)
8. Gray, C., Radford, A.: Using electronic health records to explore negotiations around euthanasia decision making for dogs and cats in the UK. Vet. Rec. **190**(9), e1379 (2022)
9. Hanauer, D.A., et al.: Describing the relationship between cat bites and human depression using data from an electronic health record. PLoS ONE **8**(8), e70585 (2013)
10. Kass, P.H., et al.: Syndromic surveillance in companion animals utilizing electronic medical records data: development and proof of concept. PeerJ **4**, e1940 (2016)
11. Kim, E., et al.: Major medical causes by breed and life stage for dogs presented at veterinary clinics in the republic of Korea: a survey of electronic medical records. PeerJ **6**, e5161 (2018)
12. Krone, L.M., Brown, C.M., Lindenmayer, J.M.: Survey of electronic veterinary medical record adoption and use by independent small animal veterinary medical practices in Massachusetts. J. Am. Vet. Med. Assoc. **245**(3), 324–332 (2014)
13. Le, H.T., et al.: Patient-chain: patient-centered healthcare system a blockchain-based technology in dealing with emergencies. In: Shen, H., et al. (eds.) PDCAT 2021. LNCS, vol. 13148, pp. 576–583. Springer, Cham (2022). https://doi.org/10.1007/978-3-030-96772-7_54
14. Le, H.T., et al.: BloodChain: a blood donation network managed by blockchain technologies. Network **2**(1), 21–35 (2022)
15. Le, H.T., et al.: Medical-waste chain: a medical waste collection, classification and treatment management by blockchain technology. Computers **11**(7), 113 (2022)
16. Menéndez, S., et al.: Data quality of animal health records on swiss dairy farms. Vet. Rec. **163**(8), 241–246 (2008)
17. Quintana, G.N., Esteban, S.: Exploratory analysis of animal bites events in the city of buenos aires using data from electronic health records. In: Digital Personalized Health and Medicine, pp. 1283–1284. IOS Press (2020)
18. Quynh, N.T.T., et al.: Toward a design of blood donation management by blockchain technologies. In: Gervasi, O., et al. (eds.) ICCSA 2021. LNCS, vol. 12956, pp. 78–90. Springer, Cham (2021). https://doi.org/10.1007/978-3-030-87010-2_6
19. Romar, A.: Fine-grained access control in an animal health record, Ph. D. thesis, Wien (2018)

20. Sánchez-Vizcaíno, F., et al.: Demographics of dogs, cats, and rabbits attending veterinary practices in great Britain as recorded in their electronic health records. BMC Vet. Res. **13**, 1–13 (2017)
21. Singleton, D.A., et al.: Pharmaceutical prescription in canine acute Diarrhoea: a longitudinal electronic health record analysis of first opinion veterinary practices. Front. Vet. Sci. **6**, 218 (2019)
22. Son, H.X., Le, T.H., Quynh, N.T.T., Huy, H.N.D., Duong-Trung, N., Luong, H.H.: Toward a blockchain-based technology in dealing with emergencies in patient-centered healthcare systems. In: Bouzefrane, S., Laurent, M., Boumerdassi, S., Renault, E. (eds.) MSPN 2020. LNCS, vol. 12605, pp. 44–56. Springer, Cham (2021). https://doi.org/10.1007/978-3-030-67550-9_4
23. Son, H.X., Nguyen, M.H., Vo, H.K., Nguyen, T.P.: Toward an privacy protection based on access control model in hybrid cloud for healthcare systems. In: Martínez Álvarez, F., Troncoso Lora, A., Sáez Muñoz, J.A., Quintián, H., Corchado, E. (eds.) CISIS/ICEUTE -2019. AISC, vol. 951, pp. 77–86. Springer, Cham (2020). https://doi.org/10.1007/978-3-030-20005-3_8
24. Summers, J.F., et al.: Health-related welfare prioritisation of canine disorders using electronic health records in primary care practice in the UK. BMC Vet. Res. **15**, 1–20 (2019)
25. Thi, Q.N.T., Dang, T.K., Van, H.L., Son, H.X.: Using JSON to specify privacy preserving-enabled attribute-based access control policies. In: Wang, G., Atiquzzaman, M., Yan, Z., Choo, K.-K.R. (eds.) SpaCCS 2017. LNCS, vol. 10656, pp. 561–570. Springer, Cham (2017). https://doi.org/10.1007/978-3-319-72389-1_44
26. Tulloch, J., et al.: The passive surveillance of ticks using companion animal electronic health records. Epidemiol. Infect. **145**(10), 2020–2029 (2017)

Difficulties and Solutions for Industrial Data Security and Compliance Governance

Zhongqi Guan[✉]

Ernst & Young (China) Advisory Limited, Beijing 100010, China
guanlegal@163.com

Abstract. With the rapid development of emerging digital technologies such as big data, 5G and cloud computing, a technological pedestal has been built for industrial digital transformation, accelerating industrial productivity and upgrading industrial structure. However, industrial data, as a core element of digital transformation, faces great governance difficulties. Massive industrial data exists widely in industrial research and development, production, operation and other links, data security, compliance will directly affect the quality and effect of digital transformation, so industrial data processors to carry out safe and compliant data governance is a necessary initiative in the process of digital transformation, but also to fulfil the legal obligations to meet the inevitable requirements of regulatory requirements.

Keywords: Industrial data · data security · data compliance · digital transformation

1 Introductory

In the era of digital economy, data has become an important element to drive the development of various industries. In the industrial field, massive data exists in all aspects of industrial production, sales, etc. The effective use of industrial data is an important element to enhance the productivity, innovation and competitiveness of industrial enterprises. From the definition, according to the "Measures for the Management of Data Security in the Field of Industry and Information Technology (for Trial Implementation)", industrial data refers to the data generated and collected in the process of research and development and design, production and manufacturing, operation and management, operation and maintenance, and platform operation in various fields of industrial industries. From the perspective of sources, industrial data come from all aspects of "research, production, supply, marketing and service", all elements of "human, machine, material, method and environment", ERP, MES, PLC and other systems, with dimensions and complexity far exceeding those of the consumer Internet, and facing challenges such as difficulties in collection, different formats and complexity of analyses [1]. It can be seen that the many application scenarios, data types and data sources of industrial data have brought great challenges to industrial data governance. The security and compliance of industrial data is not only an important prerequisite for

M. Luo and L.-J. Zhang (Eds.): CLOUD 2023, LNCS 14204, pp. 66–75, 2024.
https://doi.org/10.1007/978-3-031-51709-9_6

the production and operation of industrial enterprises, but also an important element that affects the development of the national industrial economy, especially the important data and core data in industrial data are related to national security and economic stability. In this regard, the author combines industry best practices and laws and regulations to provide solutions for industrial data governance from the perspectives of security and compliance, starting from the three core topics of industrial data governance drivers, governance difficulties, and governance solutions.

2 Presentation of the Issue

Under the influence of the new round of scientific and technological revolution and industrial revolution, the changes in innovation organisation and industrial organisation have led to changes in the structure of the innovation system, and digital innovation elements have become the focus of the governance of the innovation ecosystem [2]. Data has become one of the important factors of production [3]. Profoundly affecting the digital transformation process, industrial data has been generating significant benefits in production, sales and supply chain in industrial digital transformation; however, along with the development, there is a need to strengthen the governance of data security and compliance.

2.1 National Policy

In 2020, the Ministry of Industry and Information Technology (MIIT) issued the "Ministry of Industry and Information Technology's Guiding Opinions on the Development of Industrial Big Data" (hereinafter referred to as "Opinions"), which points out that it promotes the convergence and sharing of industrial data, deepens the integration and innovation of data, improves the data governance capacity, strengthens the management of data security, and endeavours to create a resource-rich, application-rich, industrially advanced, and governance-organized industrial big data ecosystem. The Opinions succinctly point out that while promoting the prosperous development of industrial data, it is also necessary to carry out data governance activities and strengthen data security management, in addition to carrying out data compliance activities in accordance with laws, regulations and industry standards.

2.2 The Internal and External Environment of the Enterprise

From the internal point of view, the development of industrial big data is an important part of the digital transformation of industry and the application of big data, after years of development, China's industrial Internet has made significant progress in the improvement of the system architecture, platform system construction, industrial software research and development, marking and resolution layout, enterprise application practice and security construction, etc., but the application of industrial data is still in the exploratory stage [4]. In the exploratory phase, but it also happens to be the optimal phase for governance of industrial data, where data governance norms help to improve data quality [5]. Provide a good foundation for the application of data. Externally, industrial data to carry out security and compliance governance is also based on the need for external regulation and external threats.2023 In February 2023, the National Industrial Information Security Development and Research Centre released the "2022 Industrial Information Security Posture Report", which shows that in 2022, ransomware attacks continued to threaten industrial information security, the impact of industrial data leakage incidents further expanded, and supply chain attacks exacerbated security threats. Meanwhile, with the promulgation of laws and regulations such as the Regulations on the Administration of Critical Information Infrastructure Security (for Trial Implementation) and the Data Security Law, the Ministry of Industry and Information Technology (MIIT), the Office of Internet Information Office (OIIO), and other regulatory bodies, have increased the supervision of industrial data-related enterprises. Finally, in terms of industrial industrial development, creating an industrial big data product and service system and focusing on building an industrial data innovation ecosystem are important measures to stimulate the potential of industrial data resource elements and accelerate the development of industrial big data industry. To this end, it is necessary to escort the development of industrial industry and industrial digital transformation around industrial data by clarifying the main responsibility of enterprises and building a system of industrial data security and compliance.

2.3 The Legal Obligation

China has gradually clarified the security and compliance obligations of enterprises as data processors through legislation. In terms of civil law, the General Principles of the Civil Law of 2017 clarifies that the personal information of natural persons is subject to legal protection, and Title IV, Chapter 6 of the Civil Code of 2020, entitled "Privacy and Personal Information Protection", includes personal information rights and interests as an important part of the protection of the basic civil legislation, and requires that natural persons, legal persons, and unincorporated organisations all have to Natural persons, legal persons and unincorporated organisations are all required to fulfil their obligations to protect the personal information of natural persons, otherwise they will be subject to civil legal liability. In terms of administrative laws, the Cybersecurity Law adopted in 2016, together with the Data Security Law and the Personal Information Protection Law adopted in 2021, constitute China's administrative legal system in the field of data security and protection, which is regulated by the State Net Information Department, the Industry and Information Technology Department and the State Public Security Department. In terms of criminal law, the Criminal Law Amendment (VII) adopted in 2009 explicitly stipulates the criminal liability for stealing, illegally obtaining, selling and illegally providing citizens' personal information, and the Criminal Law Amendment (IX) adds the crime of refusing to fulfil the obligation of information network security management, which opens up a new path of criminal liability for network service providers by failing to fulfil the legal obligation of acting as the responsibility model of the platform [6]. In addition, based on the characteristics of industrial data, the Ministry of Industry and Information Technology (MIIT) and other ministries and commissions have issued regulations and normative documents such as Several Provisions on the Safety Management of Automotive Data (for Trial Implementation), Measures for Cybersecurity

Review, and Measures for the Management of Data Security in the Field of Industry and Information Technology (for Trial Implementation). The aforementioned legal documents build a data security and compliance obligation and regulatory framework for industrial data processors.

3 The Governance Difficulties of Industrial Big Data Security and Compliance Governance

In 2015, the State Council released "Made in China 2025", less than two years from the implementation of China's programme of action for the first decade of the strategy of manufacturing a strong country, industrial data empowered industrial development, will provide a strong impetus for the implementation of China's strategy of manufacturing a strong country, and the governance of industrial data is imminent. The author analyses industrial data quality, data security and governance basis from three perspectives, aiming to clarify the difficult issues and the direction of governance.

3.1 Low Data Quality

At present, some enterprises in China's industrial field still have paper-based office, paper-based records of production data, resulting in a large amount of industrial data belongs to the unstructured data, increasing the difficulty of data governance; enterprises in the introduction of production systems or technologies, the lack of data development and utilization of pre-design, resulting in the collection of data, storage and other processing behaviours chaotic; in the area of production management, the enterprise for industrial data quality improvement does not focus on "management", but generally stay in the "technical" level of discussion. In terms of production management, enterprises do not pay attention to "management", but generally stay in the "technical" level of discussion [7]. As a result, the phenomenon of data isolation is created, which also buries hidden dangers for data security; in addition, enterprises lack the management of data timeliness, and do not establish a data quality system related to analyses to decide which parts of the data should be archived and which parts should be deleted, resulting in a large amount of data extrusion and the emergence of data "rotting buildings", and "the more data there is, the more responsibility it takes", which will bring great pressure on the data security of the enterprise and the governance of compliance.

3.2 Poor Data Security Environment

In recent years, China's industrial development has been rapid, but the industrial data security environment is still harsh. Industry involves many specific industries such as energy, steel, machinery, chemical industry, etc., which meets the 4V characteristics of big data [8], Volume, velocity, variety, Veracity. in addition, industrial data is associated with national critical information infrastructure in important industries and fields such as public communications and information services, energy, transportation, water conservancy, national defence science and technology industry; the higher the degree of networked intelligence of these important information systems and infrastructures, the more fragile their security becomes [9]. According to the 2022 Industrial Information Security Posture Report, in 2022, there were 89 publicly disclosed ransom times in the industrial sector; Verizon's 2022 Data Breach Investigations Report shows that in 2022, there were 338 data breaches in the manufacturing sector, an increase of 25.2% over last year. Therefore, there is an urgent need to carry out industrial data security and compliance governance, so that industrial data is safe and available to empower enterprise development.

3.3 Lack of Governance Basis

Throughout the law, there are no special laws, regulations and administrative rules for the field of industrial big data, and the legal compliance responsibility can only be sorted out based on the Network Security Law, the Regulations on the Security Protection of Critical Information Infrastructure (for Trial Implementation), and the Data Security Law, etc., and there is a lack of specialised legislation, and the Guidelines on the Classification and Hierarchy of Industrial Data (for Trial Implementation), as a guiding document on the classification and hierarchical protection of industrial data, does not have the Legal effect [10]. In addition, in October 2021, the Central Committee of the Communist Party of China and the State Council issued the Outline for the Development of National Standardisation, which explicitly mentions that it is necessary to establish standards for the industrial Internet, formulate innovative infrastructure standards to support scientific research, technological research and development, and product development, and promote the transformation and upgrading of traditional infrastructure. The introduction of the policy reflects the fact that China's industrial Internet platform is facing the thorny issue of standardisation, and the lack of standards to support the application layer, data layer and resource layer has led to "information islands" and "data chimneys" [11]. In summary, the lack of specialised and authoritative guidelines in conducting industrial data governance, both at the legal level and at the standards level, creates a great deal of uncertainty for enterprises in conducting industrial data security and compliance governance.

4 Governance Programme for Industrial Data Security and Compliance Governance

The governance of industrial data needs to build a foundation for industrial data governance with laws and regulations as the core and network security and data compliance as the two wings. Before carrying out industrial data governance, legal and regulatory requirements should first be sorted out to clarify the legal baseline from the perspective of cybersecurity and data compliance; according to the legal baseline, the management system and technical system should be constructed; then risk rectification and capacity enhancement should be carried out around the life cycle of the data; it is also necessary to carry out audits of cybersecurity and compliance in order to verify the effect and implementation. At the same time, it is also necessary to fulfil the obligation to protect personal information.

4.1 Clear Legal Baseline

The first task of data governance is to carry out the combing of laws and regulations to clarify the legal obligations and responsibilities required. By combing the requirements of laws and regulations such as the Cybersecurity Law, Regulations on the Security and Protection of Critical Information Infrastructure, and the Data Security Law, it can also serve as a material for self-certification of compliance in the event of regulation or disputes. When sorting out the legal baseline, it is important to comply not only with laws and regulations, but also with local rules and regulations as well as relevant foreign acts. At the business level, it is also necessary to focus on business-centred legal systems, for example, for the cross-border field of industrial data, it is also necessary to meet norms such as the Data Cross-Border Impact Assessment, and where personal information is involved, it is also necessary to meet the special provisions of the Personal Information Protection Act.

4.2 Constructing Management and Technical Systems

After completing the legal baseline, legal and regulatory obligations need to be integrated into the enterprise's management system, governance processes, necessary actions, etc. to meet legal and regulatory requirements. From the perspective of management system, enterprises need to establish corresponding organisational and institutional measures; for example, according to the provisions of the Network Security Law, enterprises need to fulfil the obligations of network security level protection, monitoring, early warning and emergency response, and protection of users' personal information. According to the provisions of the Data Security Law, enterprises need to perform data classification and protection, data life-cycle processing activities, risk monitoring and assessment obligations, important data and core data catalogue filing, and so on. In response to the above obligations, enterprises need to set up security and compliance organisations, such as security and compliance committees, and clarify the content of their responsibilities. From the viewpoint of technical system, enterprises need to carry out monitoring and recording network operation status, especially for security events, authority classification, access control, etc.; in addition, they also need to build up network security protection technology, alarm and warning, data encryption, remote erase, identity authentication, desensitisation and other technologies to ensure that certain data security objectives are achieved, the core of which include confidentiality, integrity, availability, controllability and non-repudiation. Security objectives of confidentiality, integrity, availability, controllability and non-repudiation [12].

4.3 Data Lifecycle Governance

According to the Data Security Act and the model (Data Security Capability Maturity Mode, DSMM) the data lifecycle can be divided into six stages, which are data collection, data storage, data transmission, data processing, data exchange and data destruction. The author briefly analyses the following stages, firstly, in the collection process, there are many sources of industrial data, and the data sources of big data are diversified, including databases, text, pictures, videos, web pages and other types of structured, unstructured and semi-structured data. Therefore, the first step of big data processing is to collect data from data sources and carry out pre-processing operations to provide a unified and high-quality data set for subsequent processes [13]. When collecting, safe technical means should be adopted to collect structured data; according to the way of collection, it can be specifically divided into direct collection and indirect collection, and indirect collection also needs to clarify the relevant rights and obligations, especially the security responsibility obligations. Secondly, in the storage link, the data should be graded and classified, and the protection of important data and core data should be strengthened; it is also necessary to back up the data, and make clear the scope and frequency of back up, etc. When cloud storage technology is used, it can be stored in the form of multi-copy, multi-node and distributed storage, and if it is stored in the physical storage, it is necessary to guarantee the security of the physical storage environment as well as the control of authority. In addition, in the transmission link, the transmission should be carried out in a safe and trustworthy way, and access control, legitimacy review, registration and approval, transmission records, contract signing, acceptance and checking, and other technologies or systems should be established to comprehensively guarantee the security and legitimacy of the data transmission; and at the same time, it is necessary to pay attention to the cross-border behaviour of data, and Articles 11, 24, 25, 26, 31, 36, etc. of the Data Security Law regulate the behaviour of data Cross-border flow behaviour is regulated, and enterprises need to clarify the legal obligations, determine the scope of cross-border data, and establish a cross-border assessment mechanism when implementing it. Finally, in the destruction link, enterprises should establish data deletion strategy and management system, clarify the requirements of deletion object, process and technology, etc., and at the same time record the destruction activities, and verify the destruction and results; it is also necessary to note that the data stored in electronic and other related forms may be stored in different terminals or systems, so it is necessary to carry out all-around verification; if physical destruction is adopted, it may be adopted by means of a shredder or a crusher If physical destruction is adopted, a shredder or crusher can be used to ensure that the destruction is thorough and irrecoverable.

4.4 Emergency Management and Data Audit

Enterprises should establish an emergency management system and a data security audit system. The external security environment of industrial data is harsh, and an emergency response plan for security incidents should be formulated; when a security threat leads to an abnormality or malfunction of the industrial control system, emergency protective measures should be taken immediately to prevent the situation from expanding, and reported level by level up to the local provincial department in charge of industry and information technology. The data security audit system has been formed for a long time, and the Guiyang City Big Data Security Management Regulations, released in 2018, state that the unit responsible for security should establish a big data security audit system, stipulate the audit workflow, and carry out regular security audits and analysis work. Taking data in the cloud as an example, cloud data is exposed to different kinds and degrees of security risks at all stages, and data security audits should be conducted around the five stages of the data lifecycle hosted in the cloud, i.e., generation, storage, use, archiving, and destruction (recycling) [14].

4.5 Obligation to Protect Personal Information in the Governance Process

In the process of industrial data governance, personal information will be highly involved in the process of data governance, and the key is human intelligence and human utilisation of technology. During the development of Germany's Industry 4.0, security aspects as well as data privacy issues were mentioned several times, suggesting that the privacy of personal data needs to be investigated more in the era of Industry 4.0 [15]. At the same time, the collection of personal information will never diminish as the industrial revolution demands higher levels of data collection and improved user experience [16]. The protection of personal information is indispensable in the governance of industrial data. On the basis of the above governance programme, and in accordance with China's existing laws and regulations, enterprises also need to strengthen the classification and management of personal information, especially the management of sensitive personal data; as well as to adopt corresponding encryption, de-identification and other security technology measures; to reasonably determine the authority of the personnel to handle personal information processing, and to conduct regular security education and training for practitioners. In addition, it is necessary to establish a system for assessing the impact of personal information security, a mechanism for responding to the rights of the subject of personal information, and a compliance process for cross-border transmission and entrusted processing to ensure that personal information is handled in a safe and compliant manner.

4.6 Special Governance of Important Data and Core Data

The Measures for the Management of Data Security in the Field of Industry and Information Technology (for Trial Implementation), which was formally implemented on 1 January 2023, sets out a number of requirements for data processors in the field of industry and information technology in relation to the security and compliance obligations for important and core data. In addition, according to Articles 21, 27, 30, 31 and 46 of the Data Security Law, the statutory obligations and legal liabilities of important data processors are stipulated, which include, inter alia, the development of important data catalogues and strengthening of their protection, the clarification of the person responsible for security and the management agency, the conduct of regular assessments of the data processing activities and the reporting to the competent authorities, and the obligations of cross-border security of important data and liabilities in case of violation of the law. Meanwhile, Articles 21 and 45 provide for the identification of core data, a strict protection system and liability for violations of the law. In summary, China has stipulated security and compliance obligations at the legislative level for industrial enterprises as processors of industrially important data and core data. On the basis of the above governance scheme, for the security and compliance governance of important data and core data, the first step should be to carry out classification and grading work and formulate a data catalogue in accordance with norms such as the "Rules for the Identification of Important and Core Data in the Industrial Sector (Draft)", and to classify the data according to different categories, attributes and interrelationships based on a certain classification principle, and to classify data in different categories according to the degree of their impact on national security, people's interests, etc., and classify different types of data according to their impact on national security, people's interests, etc. [17]. According to the "Data Security Protection Requirements for Industrial Enterprises (Draft)", the security protection work is carried out for different levels of industrial data, and the national standards such as the "Basic Requirements for the Security Management of Industrial Control Systems" are referred to to carry out the security management for industrial control systems. Secondly, industrial enterprises should strengthen the research and development of industrial data security technology, especially for database boundary protection, authority authentication, invasion vulnerability detection, data encryption and desensitisation and other technologies need to build a complete technical protection system to ensure data security. Finally, in the processing of important data and core data should be in line with the fulfilment of legal obligations, for example, according to the "Measures for the Security Assessment of Data Exit", the data exit should be declared through the local provincial net credit department to the national net credit department for the security assessment of data exit.

5 Conclusion

China's economy has shifted from the stage of high-speed growth to the stage of high-quality development, and China's industrial development is also in the critical period of transforming the development mode, optimising the economic structure, and transforming the growth momentum. The environment, conditions, methods and goals of industrial development are undergoing profound changes, and the creative use of industrial data to empower production and operation is on the rise. This paper describes the security and compliance governance motivations, governance difficulties, and governance solutions for industrial data, and provides decision-making references for enterprises to rationally develop and use industrial data, optimise production processes, and promote digital transformation. However, this paper only analyses industrial data governance solutions from the perspective of security and compliance, and does not give comprehensive suggestions in the context of national policy, technology development, talent strategy, etc. Secondly, this paper is only based on the current best practices and legal regulations, which is difficult to meet the dynamic development needs of industrial data.

References

1. Gang, G., Chao, Y., Tang, P., Ye, L.: Industrial Data Governance Practice Based on industrial data governance practices based on business value. Information Engineering (2022)
2. Adner, R.: Ecosystem as Structure. J. Manage. **43**(1), 39–58 (2017)
3. Wang, J.: An overview of industrial big data technologie. Big Data (2017)
4. Wu, H.: Digital Opportunity and Innovation Ecology. Science and Technology Herald (2021)
5. Bhansali, N.: Data governance: Creating value from information assets. CRC Press (2013)
6. Liu, S.: On Data Processors' Important Data Security Protection Obligations and Criminal Liability, Beijing Social Science (2022)
7. Li, J., Huang, Z., Liang, Z.: Industrial Data Governance: Core Issues, Transformation Logic and Research Framework. Research in Science (2022)
8. Manyyika, J., Chuim, M.,Brown, B.: Bigdata: the next frontier for innovation , competition, and productivity (2011)

9. Wu, S.: Security risks and policy choices in the era of big data. China's information security (2013)
10. Liu, M., Sheng, H.: Analysis of laws and regulations on Industrial data security protection in China. Network security and data governance (2022)
11. Industrial Internet Research Group of Wuhan University: Strategic thinking on the high-quality development of industrial Internet during the 14th Five-Year Plan period. Soft Science of China (2020)
12. Wang, B., Ji, Z.: Research on information security technology system. Computer application (2009)
13. Feng, D., Min, Z., Hao, L.: Big data security and privacy protection. J. Comput. Sci. (2014)
14. Yux, W.: A view about cloud data security from data life cycle. In: International Conference on Computational Intelligence and Software Engineering (2010)
15. Onik, M.M.H., Ahmed, M.: Blockchain in the Era of Industry 4.0. In: Data Analytics, CRC Press (2018)
16. Onik, M.M.H., Chul-Soo, K.I.M., Yang. J.: Personal data privacy challenges of the fourth industrial revolution. In: International Conference on Advanced Communications Technology(ICACT) (2019)
17. Yong, Z.: Criminal law protection of data security classification classification. Rule of Law Research (2021)

Exploration and Practice of Blockchain Universal On-Chain Data Structure in Business Systems

Bin Tang[✉]

Inesa Intelligent Tech INC., Shanghai 200233, China
tangb@inesa-it.com

Abstract. Blockchain, with its distributed, transparent, and tamper resistant characteristics, can effectively build a trust and collaboration network when facing data assetization, which is the process of transforming data into valuable assets. Blockchain can perfectly meet the needs of data confirmation, orderly circulation, and transparent supervision in various domains and scenarios. At the same time, the demand for blockchain technology for important business data applications in various industries is also increasing rapidly. However, from classic scenarios of blockchain applications, such as cryptocurrency and smart contracts, it has been found that the structure of transaction data stored on blockchain is relatively simplified and standardized. The difficulty of implementing solutions to enable blockchain to carry various complex business data with different formats and requirements can be imagined. Therefore, in the practice of blockchain technology in general business systems, the design of on-chain data structures, which are the ways to encode and store business data on blockchain, often becomes crucial and challenging. By practicing the scenario of "infectious disease report card" certificate storage and query, which is a use case of blockchain for public health management, we attempt to summarize a universal uplink structure to guide general business systems in implementing key business data blockchain solutions effectively and efficiently.

Keywords: Blockchain · On-chain data structure · Infectious disease report card

1 Introduction

With the advent of Data assets recorded into the balance sheet, data, as an asset and production factor, is incorporated into the economic accounting system, reflecting the core value and contribution of data in digital transformation. In order to better utilize and protect data assets, various industries need to accelerate the processing of data asset technology, improve the credibility, security, and liquidity of data. Blockchain technology, as an innovative distributed ledger technology, has the characteristics of decentralization, tamper resistance, and traceability, meeting some key requirements for data asset processing. Therefore, it will become a trend for more and more important data in business systems to be linked up.

© The Author(s), under exclusive license to Springer Nature Switzerland AG 2024
M. Luo and L.-J. Zhang (Eds.): CLOUD 2023, LNCS 14204, pp. 76–84, 2024.
https://doi.org/10.1007/978-3-031-51709-9_7

Looking back at the origin of blockchain technology, it can be traced back to 1991 when two computer scientists, Stuart Hubble and W. Scott Stonatta, proposed a timestamp based digital signature method that can link multiple documents into an immutable chain. This method, known as the Hubble Stonatta chain, can be seen as the embryonic form of blockchain technology. In 2008, a mysterious figure pseudonym Nakamoto published a paper proposing a decentralized electronic currency system based on cryptography and distributed consensus, known as Bitcoin. Bitcoin is one of the earliest and most successful applications of blockchain technology, which enables decentralized currency issuance and trading through blockchain.

From classic scenarios of blockchain applications, it has been found that the transaction data structure stored on blockchain is relatively simple, mainly including information such as transaction parties, transaction amount, and transaction time. This information is sufficient to ensure the effectiveness and completeness of transactions, but for other types of business data, more details and metadata may be required. For example, in supply chain management, in addition to transaction information, it is also necessary to record information such as the source, flow direction, quality, and quantity of goods; In the field of healthcare, in addition to the interaction information between patients and doctors, it is also necessary to record the patient's medical history, diagnosis, treatment, medication, and other information; In the field of education and training, in addition to transaction information between learners and educational institutions, it is also necessary to record learners' learning progress, grades, certificates, and other information. These business data often have complex structures and formats, and if stored directly on the blockchain, it can lead to issues such as excessive burden, low efficiency, and high costs.

Therefore, when implementing business data on-chain, it is necessary to consider how to design a reasonable and effective on-chain structure, which can ensure the credibility and security of data on the blockchain, as well as the availability and flexibility of data in the business system. This article aims to explore the practice of blockchain on chain structure in business systems, and analyze the problems and challenges through examples of on chain scenarios, attempting to summarize a universal on chain structure, thereby guiding general business systems to implement key business data blockchain solutions.

2 Blockchain Requirements for Business Systems

Considering the use of block chain technology business system, we often face the challenges of lack of trust, security risks and inefficiency, which are manifested in:

1. Because there may be conflicts of interest or competition among business system participants, they often lack mutual trust. It needs to rely on third-party institutions or intermediaries to provide trust services, such as certification, auditing, arbitration and so on. These third-party organizations or intermediaries may have problems such as abuse of power, opaque information, inefficiency or high cost. Affect the fairness and reliability of the business system.

2. Because the exchange of data and information between participants needs to be carried out through a centralized server or database, These servers or databases may be subject to threats such as hacker attacks, data leakage, data tampering, or data loss. Affect the security and integrity of business systems.
3. Because the exchange of data and information among participants needs to follow complex business processes and rules, These business processes and rules may involve multiple steps, multiple links, multiple departments, or multiple organizations. Resulting in low efficiency, high latency, or high errors in business systems.

Through the application of block chain technology, the following advantages can be provided for these business systems:

- Improve trust: Blockchain technology enables decentralized storage and sharing of data. It enables participants to trust and collaborate with each other without relying on third-party institutions or intermediaries. Blockchain technology uses cryptographic algorithms to guarantee the encryption, signature, verification and hashing of data, preventing data from being tampered with or forged. Block chain technology uses distributed consensus mechanism to realize the collaboration and decision-making of nodes in the network. Ensure the consistency and correctness of the block-chain.
- Secure: Blockchain technology can take advantage of its distributed and decentralized nature to protect against a single point of failure or attack. And the stability and the reliability of the network are improved. Block chain technology can record the history of data and information exchange by using its characteristics of non-tampering and traceability. Improve the auditability and verifiability of data.
- Enhance automation: Blockchain technology can utilize smart contracts to automate the processing of data and business logic. Reduce manual intervention and errors, and improve the speed and accuracy of business processes. Smart contract is a kind of code written and executed on the block chain. It can trigger and execute corresponding operations according to preset conditions and rules. Such as data storage, data validation, data transfer, data rewards, etc.

3   On-Chain Data Structure is the Key to Blockchain Implementation

How to implement the blockchain in combination with the business system? The problem of business data on-chain structure cannot be avoided. As we all know, blockchain was originally used in the field of financial transactions, and the transaction information stored on the chain is relatively small. However, the main business data in the business system is often complex in structure, and these data are directly put on the block chain. It will inevitably make the data on the chain bloated, cause various processing efficiency problems, and ultimately lead to poor implementation experience. Therefore, the design of the on-chain structure has become a key task for the successful implementation of the blockchain.

3.1   Example of On-Chain Scenario

In order to facilitate the explanation, the author will take the declaration of infectious diseases as an example, and the block chain plays a role in reporting and depositing certificates in the declaration. As shown in the figure below, the infectious disease report card is generally composed of personal basic in-formation, case information and related supplementary card information. The information composition is complex and the input items are numerous (Fig. 1).

传染病报告卡

(2023 年版)

卡片编号：_____   报卡类别：1、初次报告   2、订正报告(A、变更诊断；B、死亡；C、填卡错误)

患者姓名*：_____（患儿家长姓名：_____）
有效证件号：□□□□□□□□□□□□□□□□□□   性别：□男 □女
出生日期*：_____年____月____日（如出生日期不详，实足年龄：_____ 年龄单位：□岁□月□天）
工作单位或学校或托幼机构*：_____   联系电话：_____
病人属于*：□本县区 □本市其他县区 □本省其它地市 □外省 □港澳台 □外籍
现住址（详填）*：_____省_____市_____县（区）_____乡（镇、街道）_____村_____（门牌号）
患者职业*：
□幼托儿童、□散居儿童、□学生（大中小学）、□教师、□保育员及保姆、□餐饮食品业、□商业服务、□医务人员、□工人、□民工、
□农民、□牧民、□渔（船）民、□干部职员、□离退人员、□家务及待业、□其他（_____）、□不详
病例分类*：(1) □疑似病例、□临床诊断病例、□确诊病例、□病原携带者
　　　　　(2) □急性、□慢性（乙型肝炎、丙型肝炎、血吸虫病填写）
发病日期*：_____年____月____日（病原携带者填初检日期或就诊时间）
诊断日期*：_____年____月____日____时   死亡日期：_____年____月____日____时

甲类传染病*：□鼠疫、□霍乱

乙类传染病*：
□传染性非典型肺炎、艾滋病（□HIV 阳性、□艾滋病）、病毒性肝炎（□甲型、□乙型、□丙型、□丁型、□戊型、□未分型）、□脊髓灰质炎、□人感染高致病性禽流感、□麻疹、□流行性出血热、□狂犬病、□流行性乙型脑炎、□登革热、疟疾（□间日疟、□恶性疟、和）分型）、病痢（□细菌性、□阿米巴性）、肺结核（□涂阳肺结核、□病原学阳性、□仅胸片阳性、□未痰检）、伤寒（□伤寒、□副伤寒）、流行性脑脊髓膜炎、□百日咳、□白喉、□新生儿破伤风、□猩红热、□布鲁氏菌病、□淋病、梅毒（□I 期、□II 期、□III 期、□胎传、□隐性）、□钩端螺旋体病、□血吸虫病、疟疾（□间日疟、□恶性疟、□未分型）、□人感染 H7N9 禽流感、□新冠病毒感染

丙类传染病*：
□流行性感冒、□流行性腮腺炎、□风疹、□急性出血性结膜炎、□麻风病、□流行性和地方性斑疹伤寒、□黑热病、□包虫病、□丝虫病、□除霍乱、细菌性和阿米巴性痢疾、伤寒和副伤寒以外的感染性腹泻病、□手足口病

其他重点监测传染病*：□水痘□侵袭性肺炎□尖锐湿疣、□水痘、□肝吸虫病、□生殖道衣原体感染、□恙虫病、□森林脑炎、□人感染猪链球菌、□人粒细胞无形体病、□不明原因肺炎、□发热伴血小板减少综合征、□AFP

性病报告附卡（报告性病时须加填本栏项目）*
婚姻状况*：□未婚 □已婚有配偶 □离异或丧偶 □不详
文化程度*：□文盲 □小学 □初中 □高中或中专 □大专及以上
接触史*：□注射毒品史、□非婚性性接触史、□配偶/固定性伴阳性、□男男性行为史、□献血（浆）史、□输血/血制品史、□母亲阳性、□职业暴露史、□手术史、□其他（_____）、□不详
感染途径*：□注射毒品、□非婚性传播、□同性传播、□性接触-注射毒品史、□献血（浆）、□输血/血制品、□母婴传播、□职业暴露、□其他、□不详
样本来源*：□术前检测、□受血前检测、□性病门诊、□其他就诊者检测、□婚前检测、□孕前检查、□其他（_____）

乙肝病例附卡（报告乙肝时填本栏项目）
HBsAg 阳性时间：○>6 个月 ○6 个月内血阴性转为阳性 ○既往未检测或结果不详
首次出现乙肝症状和体征时间：_____年____月 □不详
本次 ALT _____U/L
抗-HBc IgM1:1000 检测结果 ○阳性 ○阴性 ○未做
肝穿刺检测结果 ○急性病变 ○慢性病变 ○未做
恢复期血清 HBsAg 阴转、抗-HBs 阳转 ○是 ○否 ○未做

订正前病名：_____   退卡原因：_____
报告单位：_____   联系电话：_____
报告医生*：_____   填卡日期*：_____年____月____日
备注：

Fig. 1. Example of Infectious Disease Report Card

In order to avoid linking the report data as a whole, the hash value is used as the characteristic value of the whole report in-formation at the beginning of the design. The obtain on-chain structure is initially defined as an on-chain data source system, an on-chain type, a report state and a report overall hash value. Based on this structure, we will find the following problems when we use the deposit evidence query scenario:

1. When querying, if the report information changes, the report cannot be found on the chain with the hash value generated by the changed report.
2. If the query is to report the information before the change, it means that the local needs to save a copy of the data before the information change every time.
3. The business system needs to record the results of each uplink query, such as whether to uplink and whether the data changes.

3.2 Introduction of Intermediate Data Structures

We are designing the database structure of the infectious disease report card, forming different tables according to the requirements of the database paradigm. Generally speaking, the information structure of infectious disease report card is composed of technical primary key, business primary key, business attributes and other parts. In order to relate the "report overall hash value" on the chain to the database row data, we introduce an intermediate data structure on the chain, This structure data is stored locally by the business system. The structure is as follows:

1. Internal Technical Number Summary

   It is used to record the technical number of the internal system and improve the query efficiency when checking information. For ex-ample: Visit ID, EMR ID.

2. Summary of concerns in the declaration system

   It is used to record the uniqueness of business ID and key in-formation of concern, such as ID card number and reported disease type.

3. Overall hash value of report information

   The hash value is generated according to the report information as a whole to store the unique information of validity, and the information is updated synchronously only when it is linked. If the hash value is used to query on the chain and no information is found, it means that there are two possibilities: the data is not linked or the data is changed.

   It is agreed that the above structural information will be generated by the business system when it is linked, and it is necessary to pay attention to the content of "Summary of Concern in the Declaration System". It is necessary to communicate with the responsible party of the "declaration system" and agree on a limited number. Because this information will be used as the content of the chain, and it is also the key content of the information query on the chain. Have a negative effect on on-chain query and storage. In addition, in order to find the copy of the "Report Information Whole" when data uploaded into blockchain, two schemes are provided here:

1. Store the Copy Number in the Internal Tech Number Summary.
2. Add the "Report information whole copy" field, for example, save the copy as a JSON object.

3.3 Optimization of On-Chain Data Structure

Combining the problem and the intermediate data structure, the on-chain structure is optimized into three types of information:

- First Type: Blockchain general information, the general key content is not limited to the following:
- The on-chain data comes from the system, such as the system number of a hospital.
- Type of on-chain business, such as infectious disease reporting
- Report status can be an option value, such as initialization, report submission, report review, and report submission.
- Second Type: Function information, predefined functions include:
- Status of the latest verification, including verification requester, verification time and verification result (consistent/inconsistent)
- Hash algorithm version that provides extensions for reporting information structure changes.
- Third Type: Evidence information:
- The declaration system pays attention to the summary, and the content is consistent with the intermediate structure.
- Report the overall hash value of the information, and the content is consistent with the intermediate structure.

As for that implementation of "the overall hash value of report information", based on the author's own experience, A hash value is typically generate based on that JSON value of the report in-formation, and it is found that if the JSON structure change, The hash value produced by that same value will be different. To solve this problem, the "hash algorithm version" field in the on-chain structure becomes necessary. This information is also an important content that needs to be agreed between the business system and the declaration system.

Then, we will sort out the processing process with the evidence query scenario, as shown in Fig. 2:

1. First, it is assumed that the block chain general class information is determined when calling the block chain interface.
2. The business systems typically initiate certificate storage query operations using a certain technical number as guiding information.
3. The business system finds the "Declaration System Attention Summary" in the intermediate structure according to a certain technical number.
4. The overall information of the report is found by the "declaration system attention summary" and the agreed "hash algorithm version", and is organized into a JSON object.
5. The business system will submit the "declaration system attention summary", "hash algorithm version" and report the overall information JSON to the blockchain system.
   ○
6. The blockchain system finds the "overall hash value of the report information" according to the "declaration system attention summary" and the "hash algorithm version".

7. The blockchain system will generate a hash value based on the overall report information JSON and the "hash algorithm version" passed over, and compare it with the "overall report information hash value" on the chain.
8. Update the comparison results to the "Last Verification Status" and return them to the business system (Fig. 2).

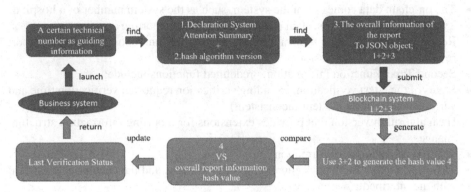

Fig. 2. Process of evidence query scenario

So far, each step of deposit inquiry has been sorted out, and the logic of the whole process is smooth.

3.4 Evolutionary Universal On-Chain Data Structure

Through the above example of "infectious disease report card", we can further evolve the structure of the chain. Apply it to general business systems (Fig. 3).

First, we need to analyze the business data and divide it into two parts:

1. Business feature information, consisting of business primary key and required information of interest, needs to be determined in limited quantity with system stakeholders.
2. Additional information, in addition to the business feature information, other information that needs to be confirmed with the relevant parties of the system.

According to the analysis of business data, the intermediate data structure is generalized as:

1. Internal Technical Number Summary

   It is used to record the technical number of the internal system, including the copy number, so as to improve the query efficiency during information checking.

2. Business characteristic information

   The service feature information from the service data sorting is used for service identifier uniqueness and key information attention.

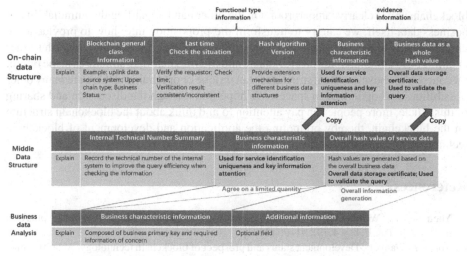

Fig. 3. Schematic diagram of Universal on-chain structure

3. Overall hash value of service data

Based on the service characteristic information and the additional information, the hash algorithm version is generated according to the convention.

Finally, the universal on-chain data structure is obtained:

- Blockchain general information, the general key content is not limited to: on-chain data source system, on-chain business type, business status, etc.
- Function type information, predefined function: latest verification status, hash algorithm version.
- The Evidence type information, including the service feature information and the overall hash value of the service data, is derived from the intermediate data structure.

4 Concluding Remarks

In summary, by sorting out the "infectious disease declaration" certificate storage query, the general data on-chain structure of the blockchain business system has been summarized, and the core information of the on-chain is the overall hash value of the business data. Storing the overall hash value of business data on the blockchain, while storing the intermediate information of business data in the blockchain docking system, minimizes the redundancy and waste of blockchain data, as well as the burden and cost of blockchain, while also ensuring the credibility and security of the data. This on-chain structure scheme allows a verifier to prove the truth of a statement to a verifier without revealing any other information.

Readers may still not understand how hash values play a role in preventing data tampering. On the one hand, this hash value serves as a verification code to indicate whether the current business data is trustworthy. This "trustworthy information" is stored on the blockchain and is clearly tamperproof. On the other hand, regarding the immutability of business data itself, we can try to transform the proposition into: how to provide a pre tampered copy of the data when data tampering occurs. This proposition is worth further exploration in combination with blockchain and intermediate data structures in the future. Of course, the above on-chain structure is not unique or optimal, and there are many other possibilities and optimization spaces. We hope that through the discussion and sharing of this article, more people can pay attention to and think about the blockchain structure on the blockchain, thereby promoting the application and development of blockchain technology in various industries.

References

1. Yuemeng, L., Wenjian, X.: Blockchain technology to improve the ability of the platform thinking. ICT & Policy **47**(9), 91–96 (2021)
2. Yong, Y., Wang, F.: Development status and prospect of blockchain technology. Acta Automat. Sinica **42**(4), 481–494 (2016)

Difficulties and Countermeasures in Data Asset Pricing

Zhuli Sai[1,2](✉) and Yunian Cheng[1,2](✉)

[1] Kunming University of Science and Technology, Kunming, China
850459368@qq.com, 415864696@qq.com
[2] South China Normal University, Guangzhou, China

Abstract. On August 16th, the Ministry of Finance issued the "Interim Regulations on the Accounting Treatment of Enterprise Data Resources Entering the Table", officially marking the beginning of data assets entering the financial accounting subject assets. Subsequently, the China Asset Appraisal Association issued the "Guiding Opinions on Data Asset Appraisal" on September 8th and confirmed its implementation from October 1st. Further guidance policies on data element rights confirmation, pricing, transaction circulation, income distribution, pilot projects, and other progress are expected to be launched one after another.

After the release of a series of policies, experts from various enterprises actively responded, researching and exploring the future market impact and implementation strategies of data policies. This is a significant benefit for enterprises with heavyweight data, as data "entering the table" will mean that the data has completed the leap from natural resources to economic assets.

But the inclusion of data assets in the table is a result, not the purpose of policies. The purpose of the policy is to promote data governance in enterprises and convert valuable data assets into actual operating income. Among them, "how to evaluate and price data assets" will become the first challenge for enterprise data resources to be included in the table.

This article will interpret the core difficulty of data asset entry into the table - "asset pricing", propose feasible response strategies and action plans, and provide direction and reference for enterprises to initiate data asset entry and data discussion.

Keywords: Data assets · Asset pricing · Data asset entry into the table

1 Difficulties in Data Asset Pricing

Data assets have the characteristic of being intangible and can be replicated at zero cost, so pricing is very difficult compared to ordinary goods. For example, evaluating a property for a certain project with a value of 2 million yuan can be considered based on conditions such as location, environment, unit type, lighting, building structure, etc. It can be evaluated through market quotations, and can also refer to the price range of surrounding properties of the same level. However, data asset pricing does not have so many explicit characteristics, and the randomness of evaluation is relatively high. Next, let's take an example of how to set rules for jewelry pricing to explain the pricing rules for data assets.

Material A1: The raw material is the price of the ore. If the same batch of jade has the same quality, the price will definitely be the same. However, after detailed classification, the price difference between good and bad carving materials of different grades immediately becomes apparent. The issue of data quality is difficult to discern at first glance, and only in the process of applying it in business scenarios can we evaluate the level of data quality.

Engraving A2: Engraving can widen the price range of jade of the same size, such as hanging pieces of the same size, which cost hundreds to thousands of yuan for good carving. Generally, it may only cost a few hundred yuan, and even worse, it may cost less than a hundred yuan. The cleaning and processing process of data is more complex and requires relative solidification, otherwise it is difficult to calculate and evaluate the amount of work generated in each link.

Polishing A3: There are two methods for polishing: one is machine brushing, which costs several tens of yuan. One method is manual polishing, which is commonly used in many high-end jade products. Pricing varies depending on the hardness of different jades, ranging from a few yuan (a finger sized jade carving costs over 5 yuan) to thousands or even tens of thousands of yuan. Due to the fact that data can be applied to different business scenarios and industries, the value that may be generated from the same data may vary. Therefore, this part of the evaluation also needs to be more targeted.

After these three evaluations, we can roughly calculate the factory price of jade: the most ordinary material, the most ordinary carving worker, and the ordinary polishing. If the raw material is 1000 yuan (depending on the actual price) + the ordinary carving worker is 500 yuan + 50 yuan for polishing, as well as various operating expenses and labor expenses, it is generally over 2000 yuan. PX pricing = A1 + A2 + A3 + market regulation.

Of course, most products use market adjusted prices. The so-called "market regulated price" refers to the commodity prices and charging standards set by producers and operators themselves, without any regulations by the state. Prices generally follow the market and fluctuate freely. If the market is prosperous, there will be demand. If there is demand in the market, it will stimulate price increases. The scarcity of certain commodities will also stimulate price increases, because "scarcity is precious" is also a market price principle.

Returning to the formulation of data asset prices, due to the special attributes of data, the pricing process becomes more complex. Firstly, the value of data is unique: the same data has different values for different scenarios, and the availability and value of different data for the same scenario are also different. For example, a certain type of power data can be applied in scenarios such as power pricing and scheduling optimization to achieve economic value; It can also be combined with financial scenarios to generate economic value for corporate financial services participating in credit evaluation; It can also be used in regional economic statistical analysis and planning decision-making models. It can be seen that for different usage scenarios, the contribution and economic value generated by the same data are different.

Secondly, data value has a synergistic characteristic: when using data, it is often found that the combination of multiple types of data produces more than the total production value of a single data in a certain scenario. This phenomenon of "1 + 1 > 2" is also a very attractive aspect of data science. Multidimensional data can more accurately assist in analyzing, predicting, and making decisions in key economic activities. Unlike traditional elements, the sum of data values cannot be linear and simple.

Finally, data value has infinite reusability: this is also a unique characteristic of data elements. Unlike traditional production factors such as land (where a house cannot be built with a parking lot, and a shopping mall cannot be built with a parking lot), data can be used by different entities at the same time to participate in multiple economic activities (of course, this requires safe and compliant use), and in this process, data has a multiplier effect on economic value. Of course, this may also lead to cost free reuse, leading to data abuse.

These data characteristics make it difficult to determine the actual value of the data, mainly reflected in the fact that data value can only generate value in corresponding scenarios. For example, there is a batch of customer loan information on the market, which can only generate income after being used by the lending enterprise, and these data assets are valuable. If a tourism enterprise buys data but provides tourism services, these data have no value to it. Therefore, this article believes that the difficulty in evaluating the value of data resources is mainly due to the following reasons: the difficulty in determining the use value of data in advance, the difficulty in evaluating data quality, unclear ownership of data assets, and the difficulty in reviewing the source of data assets.

2 Data Asset Pricing Method

Generally speaking, the value of data is divided into internal pricing and external market pricing, because many companies' data assets are not sold externally. The valuation of the value of data assets is mainly used to evaluate the value of the data department and improve enterprise efficiency. So from an internal perspective, the value evaluation and pricing of data assets are one thing, because for the enterprise itself, the value generated by data is the pricing of these data assets.

However, from an external trading perspective, the price at which these data are sold needs to be higher than their value in order to have better returns for the enterprise, and the difficulty lies here. For example, a data supplier retrieves a lot of data from some public platforms and then processes and cleans it up to form valuable data assets. The entire process costs 100000 yuan. These data need to be sold on the market and can be sold to different companies for evaluation purposes. Each data may not necessarily be 100000 yuan, but it may be priced at 50000 yuan, and in the end, 10 companies were sold; It is also possible that this part of the data is highly confidential and monopolistic, with a pricing of 500000 yuan for only one company. Regardless of the pricing method, the value of this data provider's data has generated 500000 yuan. So we can understand the pricing (or value evaluation) of data assets through two dimensions:

(1) **Pricing Within the Enterprise:** This approach is similar to value evaluation, mainly evaluating the value of the enterprise's data department and the efficiency of the enterprise's operations. Internally generated data assets collected, processed, and generated by enterprises can be preliminarily evaluated for their internal price through internal costs and benefits, which can also be understood as value, as many times internal use

may not require consideration of price. There are three common methods for evaluating the value of internal data in enterprises:

Cost method: Calculate various costs incurred during the data collection, clarity, and processing construction process, including collection costs, platform construction costs, labor costs, and so on. This solution can only reflect the cost of data assets and cannot reflect the benefits generated by the data. Therefore, if directly used for pricing, it is also a cost price, and the value of the benefits is difficult to determine.

Income method: Estimate the business income generated by the value of future data acquisition data, and consider the time value of the funds to sum up the income for each period. This method takes into account the revenue component of the cost method, but estimating revenue is a highly developed evaluation without reliable conditions to support the evaluation. For example, employees from department A of the enterprise went to the market and collected and created a batch of customer data. These customer data made it convenient for many departments to use and query data, communicate and communicate with sales, becoming potential customers. In the end, a certain sales contract of 1 million was reached in department B, and another business opportunity was found in department C. It is well-known within the enterprise that this batch of data assets generate value, but it is difficult for us to assess the revenue of this batch of data in the entire transaction. For example, if a digital department develops a data product and produces a set of data assets, which incurs costs and is provided to internal business departments of the enterprise for use, but does not directly generate revenue, how can we evaluate the value of this product in this digital department? This will directly affect the fate of this department, but there is currently no good method available. The income method clearly cannot solve this problem.

Market approach: Conduct value evaluation based on similar data already available in the market, and compare the value of the data owned by the enterprise to estimate the value of the data. The point is that it can reflect the current market situation of assets, which is more objective and more easily accepted by both parties in data trading. The difficulty lies in the professionalism and classification of these data institutions in the market. When the market is not perfect, there may not be a reasonable pricing mechanism, and even similar product data cannot be found in the market. Value is naturally difficult to evaluate.

Reverse evaluation method: It is used to evaluate the losses that may be caused to the enterprise due to low quality or incomplete data. The advantage of this method is that it considers the opportunity cost of data, and it can reverse demonstrate the importance and value of data assets to the enterprise, and even prevent risks in business operations. A way to reduce costs, for example, for a master data platform established by a certain enterprise, by uniformly recording master data supplier data, the repeated entry of suppliers in 5 departments is reduced, and the workload of user data entry is reduced. To evaluate the value brought by this work, reverse evaluation method is used. If there are 100000 supplier data, through the establishment of master data, only A department needs to uniformly input, and the other 4 departments can be connected and used, Reduce the workload of data entry, as shown in the figure:

Data Asset Value Estimation Table

Serial number	data object	Data usage department	Each data entry time	Total data volume	Accumulated time savings (working days)	Labor cost unit price (yuan/day)	Excess data entry cost (10 thousands yuan)	Data value (10 thousands yuan)
one	Supplier Master Data	Operations, Procurement, Cost, Finance	1 min	100 000	208*4	500	41.6	41.6
two								
three								

(2) External Pricing Method Between Enterprises: This pricing method is mainly used for transactions between enterprises, and the core pricing principle is the market. Establish a complete market pricing platform, mechanism, and process. A "separation of ownership and business" on the exchange data trading mechanism can be established, which means establishing a data exchange or data trading center as a third-party service institution that can only provide intermediary services for data trading, including information collection, information disclosure, information exchange, and transaction matching. Through fair and just trading, a trust mechanism between all parties in the exchange trading can be established to solve the dilemma of data resource trading. At present, this area is still in its early stages in China. As of the end of 2022, there have been over 30 data trading venues led by governments at or above the provincial level. However, foreign countries are more focused on the direction of digital currencies such as Bitcoin, and there are no good examples of data asset trading applications.

For external pricing of enterprise data assets, it can only rely on the calibration of the data trading market, and improve the mechanism of the data quotation negotiation pricing process. The data exchange establishes the corresponding data resource catalog, and the data provider is responsible for quoting. The data exchange provides certain construction suggestions and precipitates the corresponding asset catalog listing price (similar to Taobao). This trading platform can be undertaken by the government, and data demand customers can filter and negotiate based on the data resource catalog. For those with large corresponding data transaction amounts, negotiations can be conducted, and finally a data transaction contract can be signed, Determine the legal authorized entity and complete data asset transactions. With the continuous emergence of data trading, a reasonable price range for a certain type of data is gradually formed, forming a reasonable and fair pricing.

It must be mentioned here that there will be many changes in the data negotiation process, and communication between both parties is a process of commercial negotiation. There are many factors that need to be considered and influenced, including market demand, data usage, data type, usage, market demand, and data quality. These factors have a significant impact on the pricing process and need to be understood and carefully considered in advance. As follows:

- **Market demand:** The value of data is usually related to market demand. If a certain type of data has high demand in a specific industry or market, its value may be higher. For example, the financial market has a high demand for real-time stock market performance data, so this data is often valuable.

- **Purpose and benefits:** The value of data depends on the purpose it can support and the benefits it generates. If data can be used to make critical business decisions, improve products or services, improve efficiency, etc., its value will correspondingly increase. For example, customer data can be used for personalized marketing and customer retention, thereby improving sales and customer loyalty.
- **Data quality:** High quality data is usually more valuable than low-quality data. The accuracy, completeness, and timeliness of data have a significant impact on its value. Repairing inaccurate, untimely, or incomplete data may require additional costs, which reduces the value of the data.
- **Competitive environment:** The value of data is also influenced by the competitive environment. If a certain type of data is relatively scarce, it may have higher value. In some cases, competitors in the market may be willing to pay higher prices to obtain unique or exclusive data.
- **Data circulation revenue:** Some companies derive revenue from data transactions. For example, data brokers can obtain commissions or licensing fees from buying and selling data, which can also reflect the value of the data.
- **Cost benefit analysis:** Enterprises can estimate the value of data through cost benefit analysis. This includes considering the costs of data collection, processing, storage, and maintenance, and comparing them with the potential benefits of the data. For example, in the field of advertising technology, advertisers often use data to locate their target audience. A car manufacturer may be willing to pay a high price to obtain data on user purchasing tendencies and purchasing history, as this data can help them more accurately locate potential car buyers and improve the return on advertising investment.

3   Data Asset Pricing Response

Although there are currently many difficulties in evaluating data asset pricing, and the data element market is still in the normative stage. But we can still form some coping strategies to resolve these difficulties. The following are specific coping strategies:

3.1   Evaluate Intrinsic Value

Whether it is data generated within the enterprise or data purchased from data vendors, they are all data resources that the enterprise needs to mine. Usually, we will form data assets through cleaning and processing, and conduct asset inventory to form a data asset catalog. Before conducting a data asset pricing evaluation, the first step is to evaluate the potential value of these resources that have not yet formed data assets. The intrinsic value of data assets. The specific content we need to evaluate is as follows:

(1) **Data quality:** The level of data quality determines the value of assets, and the completeness, accuracy, standardization, and timeliness of data require value evaluation through an evaluation system. If the quality of data is very low, it should be removed from the asset category or asset impairment should be carried out.

(2) **Data size:** Determine the size of the data volume, such as the population data of a certain city and the population data of various cities in a certain province, which have different modulus and value.

(3) **Usage frequency:** Estimate the number of times data will be used within a certain period of time, such as daily, weekly, monthly, etc. The frequency of use and value are not necessarily related, but the higher the frequency of use, the higher its value to a certain extent, it is possible that it will be.

(4) **Service effectiveness:** Those services have been improved through data, such as reducing the workload of manual verification through high-quality data after processing and cleaning, and improving the accuracy of decision analysis, which needs to be evaluated.

In the process of conducting intrinsic value assessment, we can collect customer information, transaction information, and related information that are scattered and unused in business processes, and conduct intrinsic value assessment to evaluate the potential of this part of data assets.

3.2   Evaluate Costs and Business Value

Data that is detached from the 'scenario' cannot be evaluated for its value, so 'data + algorithms' are the means to achieve value, and the application scenario is the key to evaluating its value. When evaluating the true effectiveness of data assets, there are the following concerns:

- Focus on scenario analysis: Based on a certain business scenario, analyze the value generated during the application of statistical data;

  Focus on the end as the starting point: in the application process, reverse the value of data assets through the improvement effect;

- Focus on variable control: analyze the incremental benefits of data assets only;

  Pay attention to comprehensive consideration: evaluate the comprehensive effectiveness of data assets by combining benefits and various costs incurred in the process.

  Due to the flexibility of application scenarios, we can design scenario matrices to unify calculation methods and reduce the dimensionality of analysis content, such as vertically categorizing the value chain according to business scenarios and horizontally categorizing the value chain according to business types - the business type scenario matrix. Design a universally applicable value calculation caliber for each scenario category to calculate the total value of the scenario.

  In terms of cost value, it is necessary to consider the costs incurred in the lifecycle of data collection to application. The costs of data asset formation processes such as collection, cleaning and processing, development, operation and maintenance, and management can be aggregated to calculate their cost value.

  In terms of business value, calculate the incremental benefits of data assets through key performance indicators, and measure the empowering effect of data assets on the business. The calculation factors include transaction volume, transaction volume, total number of customers, etc. For example, the business value can be calculated through product sales, which is the "recommended transaction amount * product rate". Alternatively, the data sharing of master data can reduce the workload of previous repeated entry and verification, and improve business efficiency and value.

3.3 Evaluate Market Transaction Value

If data assets need to meet the conditions for market trading, the first thing to see is whether they can be monetized. The main focus here is to see that the part of the efficiency of data assets that can be measured in monetary terms is reflected in the economic value of data assets; The actual economic benefits obtained from trading service-oriented data assets/products in the open market are reflected in the market value of data assets.

In the process of calculating the economic value of data assets, it is still necessary to combine the application scenarios, calculate the monetized returns in the scenario value, and split the portion belonging to the data assets. When calculating the market value of data assets, refer to "transaction unit price * transaction volume" for aggregation calculation. For example, the scenario currency return calculation method for the precise recommendation list of mobile banking products is based on the transaction amount on the list * the product rate. Assuming that the application of the "precise recommendation list of mobile banking products" can increase the transaction rate by about 60%, the economic value of the list can be calculated. At the same time, by comparing the trading situation of similar algorithms or marketing insights in the market, market value can be measured and calculated.

4   Five Step Approach to Data Asset Planning

As mentioned earlier, the problems faced by data asset entry, whether it is the external market environment or internal difficulties of enterprises, are difficult to effectively solve at this stage, and corresponding regulations and policies still need to be improved and introduced as support. With policy guarantees, business operations can only be justified and justified. Only in the industry can data element ownership, pricing, transaction circulation, income distribution, and pilot projects be carried out in an orderly manner. At this time, enterprises need to improve their "internal skills" in advance, that is, establish a suitable data asset management system to enhance their data asset management capabilities; At the same time, when the country introduces corresponding policies, it can respond quickly and actively, striving for maximum benefits.

There are many prerequisites for entering data assets into the table. In addition to quantitative pricing, there should also be clear rights and responsibilities, legal and compliant data, and guaranteed data security. I believe many enterprises are pondering how to establish such a data standardization system. We conducted corresponding project practice research this time and summarized some excellent data management experiences of domestic enterprises. We have found that these enterprises have a relatively complete data governance system as their foundation. In order to enhance their data asset management capabilities, we have combined project practice to understand and organize a universal system for supporting common enterprise data asset management, abbreviated as the "Five Step Data Asset Planning Method". The introduction is as follows:

Step 1: Data asset identification and inventory: Clarifying the family background, defining, identifying, and formulating standards for assets, is the foundation for evaluating the value of data assets. Enterprises should figure out which data is of high value, which data is relatively low value, and which data needs to be mined. Only with such classification can they clarify the key driving points.

Step 2: Data Asset Usage: Statistics on the usage and frequency of data assets can provide important basis for pricing evaluation. The data usage can be listed through the data asset catalog. For assets with a usage rate of 0, whether they are useless data can be ignored. For assets with a usage rate of very high and scarce in the market, it can be considered to export to specific enterprises to obtain the maximum value return.

Step 3: Data Asset Governance: Associate with the data governance system to govern metadata, master data, data standards, and data quality. On the one hand, establish and improve the enterprise's own data standards, and on the other hand, continuously clean the data already generated by the enterprise, continuously improve data quality, ensure data security, and enhance data application value. In the process of data governance, it is necessary to establish corresponding data management organizations, attach importance to the standardization of data systems, and conduct regular assessments and drying.

Step 4: Data asset operation: Whether for internal use or external transactions, there must be long-term dedicated personnel to ensure the operation and protection of data, to ensure that problems are resolved during the use of assets, and to efficiently output data assets. At the same time, it is also conducive to the continuous appreciation and preservation of data assets, striving for excellence. Establish three standardized data asset service processes to support the standardized mechanisms, communication channels, and personnel coordination in the internal and external service processes of data assets; Establishing a data asset operation and management mechanism is mainly used to standardize the docking mechanism and operation service standards during the data usage process; Establish a data asset operation measurement system to evaluate the internal and external assessment indicators of data assets, and evaluate the level of service quality.

Step 5: Digital System Guarantee: Establish a data asset management platform, including a data service platform for data collection, data processing, data cleaning, data quality monitoring, data interface, data distribution, etc.; It also includes a data asset catalog for the data asset presentation end, such as a data catalog, a data cockpit, as well as external data trading platforms, data pricing evaluation platforms, data payment systems, and so on.

Through this **"five step method"**, the basic infrastructure for internal and external data asset transactions within the enterprise has been basically established, which meets the requirements of continuous data asset transactions. Of course, whether digital tools can be effectively utilized also requires market feedback, continuous iteration and optimization during the use process.

In general, for data assets, whether it is internal or external transactions, data pricing cannot be lacking. Otherwise, things without value are difficult to execute in the long term. At the same time, we should also deeply realize that data pricing cannot be set overnight, and we need to continuously improve, respect the market, and actively respond to market feedback. Without a perfect data pricing mechanism, all adjustment goals need to rely on this ever-changing market. Establishing fair and just data pricing standards that comply with market changes can not only provide reasonable returns for the efforts of data asset providers, but also generate business value returns for data asset demanders after using data, achieving a "win-win" situation, This data pricing mechanism can promote the long-term healthy development of data asset trading.

References

1. DMBOK2: Data Management Body of Knowledge, 2nd Edition (2009)
2. Bingrong, D., Shanshan, G., Lin, Y.: Research on Data Asset Standards Progress and suggestions. Big Data **6**(03), 36–44 (2020)
3. Adolph, M.: Bigdata, its enablers and standards. Pik Praxis Der Information sverarbeitung Und Kommunikation **37**(03), 197–204 (2014)
4. Bulger, M., Taylor, G., Schroeder, R.: Data-Driven Business Innovation, competition, and Productivity, Mc Kinsey Global Institute (2011)
5. Manyika, J., Chui, M.: Bigdata: the next frontier for innovation, competition, and productivity. Mckinsey Global Institute, pp. 1–137 (2011)
6. Tambe, P.: Big data investment, skills, and firm value. SSRN Electron. J. **60**(6), 1452–1469 (2014)
7. Sarkar, P.: Data asset management-data as a service: a framework for providing reusable enterprise data services, pp. 43–60. John Wiley & Sons, Inc., Hoboken (2015)
8. Goldstein, H., Hendriks, R.: Unplugging the DAM: making digital asset management business process based by deconstructing it. Archiving Conf. **7**(1), 28–32 (2010). https://doi.org/10.2352/issn.2168-3204.2010.7.1.art00006
9. Jessop, M.: Digital Asset Management Education and Training. Neuromuscular Disorders: Nmd **16**(4), 262–268 (2010)
10. Love, P.E.D., Zhou, J., Matthews, J., Luo, H.: Systems information modelling: enabling digital asset management. Adv. Eng. Softw. **102**, 155–165 (2016). https://doi.org/10.1016/j.advengsoft.2016.10.007
11. Wong, R.C.-W., Ada Wai-Chee, F., Wang, K., Pei, J.: Anonymization-based attacks in privacy-preserving data publishing. ACM Trans. Database Syst. **34**(2), 1–46 (2009). https://doi.org/10.1145/1538909.1538910

Author Index

M. Luo and L.-J. Zhang (Eds.): CLOUD 2023, LNCS 14204, p. 95, 2024.
https://doi.org/10.1007/978-3-031-51709-9

Printed in the United States
by Baker & Taylor Publisher Services

Printed in the United States
by Baker & Taylor Publisher Services